The Practice of Animal-Assisted Psychotherapy

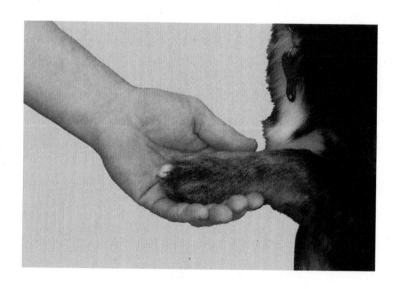

The Practice of Animal-Assisted Psychotherapy:

An Innovative Modality for Facilitating Mental Wellness

Lynn J. Piper

E Street Lane Publications LLC

E Street Lane Publications LLC
The Practice of Animal-Assisted Psychotherapy:
An Innovative Modality for Facilitating Mental Wellness
Lynn J. Piper, Ph.D.

Copyeditor: Ashleigh Imus, Ph.D.
Cover Design: Vila Design
Interior Design: Lynn J. Piper, Ph.D.

Published in the United States of America by E Street Lane Publications
LLC.

ISBN 978-0-9911867-0-9

Library of Congress Cataloging-in-Publication Data
A catalog record for this book is available from the Library of Congress

Dedication

This book is dedicated to Ian, my loving partner in life, and to Meika, Loki, Hobbes, and Zoey, the inspirations for my work. I could not do what I do without any of them.

Ian has supported me in my journey to become who I am today. He has supported me financially and, more important, emotionally as I developed into the therapist and person I am. I cannot thank him enough.

Meika, Loki, and Hobbes have all shared in the triumphs and tribulations of our clients. Just prior to publishing this book, we acquired our fourth and soon-to-be therapy dog, a Siberian husky–shepherd mix, Zoey. We have witnessed transitions through pain and suffering to self-awareness and self-growth. I could not have done it without them and truly believe that, if not for them, I would be only half the therapist I am. My therapy dogs have shown me how to be loyal, caring, and steadfast in my work with my clients and have taught me to never give up, especially when the going gets tough.

Contents

Preface

Animal-Assisted Psychotherapy: An Innovative Modality for Facilitating Mental Wellness is about how specially trained therapy dogs assist a human therapist to work with clients' mental health issues. The book's main purpose is to provide the clinical applications for animal-assisted psychotherapy (AAP). The book can be used by novices or seasoned therapists to help them understand the power of AAP and how it can be used in clinical ways to diminish mental illness symptoms, to improve a client's insight, and to aid in bringing to light clinical issues.

The book provides an introduction concerning the writer's interest in providing AAP, a history of AAP, the distinction between service dogs and therapy dogs, and the distinctions among what are considered to be animal-assisted activities, animal-assisted therapy, and animal-assisted psychotherapy. The book describes the risks and benefits of AAP, how to mitigate risks, the types of dogs that are suitable as therapy dogs, and the training they need to be considered therapy dogs. The book also describes how to determine whether therapy dogs are becoming stressed by their work and how to manage the stress. Moreover, the book discusses the ethical and legal issues related to the provision of AAP. Additionally, the book provides readers with an understanding of the many therapeutic roles a therapy dog provides or elicits for clients.

The book explores and explains how AAP can be utilized with different theoretical orientations that mental health professionals use in their work. The later chapters offer case vignettes illustrating how the therapy dog assists in the therapy process. The vignettes illustrate both planned and unplanned interventions that demonstrate how the therapy dog assists the therapist and the client. The animal-assisted interventions are directed at improving the client's symptoms related to mental illness and/or quality of life. The case vignettes focus on children, adolescents, adults, and families. Finally, the book offers previous clients' reflections on AAP and their relationship with the writer's therapy dogs.

Clinical issues addressed in the vignettes include how the therapy dog assists in establishing the therapeutic relationship, allowing the client to accept touch, processing incest, building self-esteem, mastery of frustration, becoming more aware of one's emotions, grounding, and many other important clinical issues. The book presents a broad understanding of the clinical application and power of AAP.

About the Author

Lynn J. Piper was born in London, England. She obtained her doctoral degree in clinical psychology from the University of North Texas, in Denton, Texas, USA. Since graduating and completing an internship in Dallas, Texas, and a post-doctoral residency in Fairfax, Virginia, Lynn now works in private practice in Springfield, Virginia. She specializes as an animal-assisted and trauma therapist.

Figure AA.1 Meika, Lynn, & Loki

Prior to becoming a therapist, Lynn was a police officer in England and worked as a nanny in different countries. Since becoming a therapist, she has presented at several conferences and has written articles on topics related to trauma, AAP, and AAP with trauma. Lynn has lived in England, Sweden, Canada, and the United States. She now resides contently with her partner, three dogs, and two cockatiels in Springfield, Virginia, USA.

About the Animal Co-Therapists

Meika, a golden retriever mix, and Loki, a collie mix, were both rescued from the local SPCA animal shelter in McKinney, Texas. Before they were trained and became my faithful therapy partners, both Meika and Loki were, and still are, loved family members as well as my companions and guardians when my partner is away on business trips. This book would not be possible without their efforts on behalf of my clients and me.

Meika came to us at around age 6 months. She has a beautiful golden coat on her face, back, and legs, whereas her underbelly is white. Her hair is long, and she looks much heavier and bigger than she really is. Her nose was jet black, although now graying with age, and she has exquisite black-lined eyes, something most women would be envious of, as her "makeup" looks perfect and accentuates her eyes beautifully. We were surprised at her gentle and calm demeanor. On Meika's first day with us, she was lying on the floor, and one of our cockatiel birds, a brave soul, walked over to her. Meika sniffed the bird and allowed it to "preen" her. Before we adopted Meika, my friends had warned me not to get a dog, as it would likely attack our cockatiels, who were allowed to fly and walk around our home whenever we were present. Obviously, Meika proved them wrong. This was an important sign of her accepting and tolerant nature. After we adopted Meika, we soon discovered that she was scared of large vehicles and loud noises such as thunderstorms. With time and patience, Meika has learned to be able to walk and not be startled or scared by buses or loud vehicles. Nonetheless, she has never truly gotten over her fear of thunderstorms. We do not know how her fears of noises started, but it is good to see that they are less distressing to her today.

Figure ACT.1 Meika

I had first gotten Meika as dog to run with early in the mornings in Texas, as a deterrent to any would-be attackers. Of course, if potential attackers knew her, they would know that she is more likely to lick them to death than to do any real harm.

We decided to obtain a second dog as a playmate for Meika and to keep her company while we were at work. So, Loki, our collie mix, was rescued from an SPCA animal shelter at age 10 weeks. Although many of my clients confuse Meika with Loki because they are similar in shape, Loki's colorings and markings are different. Loki's coat is mainly a biscuit color, with a white blaze down his nose, and his belly is also white. His legs and feet are predominantly white, with some biscuit-colored spots here and there. He has a long nose, which accentuates the smile he often wears.

Figure ACT.2 Loki

Loki immediately became part of our family because of his easygoing and fun nature. He loved to play with Meika, my partner, and me and was always wagging his tail. Loki also became my running mate along with Meika.

Now, as Loki ages, the only things he likes to run after are cats and squirrels when he gets the chance, although when he has cornered a cat, he merely stands there and barks at it while the cat typically swats his nose. He does occasionally "chase" clients when he reacts to their emotions. In these situations, he will typically jump on the couch and nudge or paw clients; if they do not stabilize their emotions, he will then jump down and come to me, as if to say, "do something," or "help them," which of course allows clients to discuss what is going on. In some cases, this goes on for most of the session when clients find it difficult to calm themselves or to become less agitated.

Meika and Loki were both trained and certified for animal-assisted therapy (AAT) while we were living in Texas. At the time of writing this book, animals cannot be certified for animal-assisted psychotherapy (AAP); they can only be certified for AAT. I mention this here to briefly differentiate between AAT and AAP. Much of what is done under the rubric of AAT relates more to physical therapy than to the treatment of mental health. Nonetheless, as Chapter 2 outlines in more detail, the activities of AAP fall under the definition of AAT. Thus, for the purposes of this book, I use the term "animal -assisted psychotherapy" (AAP) when I am discussing the treatment I provide to my clients.

Initially, much of Meika and Loki's AAT work involved visiting patients in the hospital. Later, as you will read further on in the book, they began to work with me in a psychotherapeutic setting. When discussing the role my dogs play for AAP, I refer to Meika, Loki, or Hobbes as my "therapy dog," "co-therapist," or as a "furry facilitator."

As Meika is now 14 years old, she has retired from her AAP work: hence, the recent adoption of Hobbes, a Lab mix. Hobbes's coloring and fur are very different from both Meika and Loki, who have long, light-colored hair that needs brushing weekly. His coloring is a "brindle" (a mix of black, brown, and tan stripes–hence the name Hobbes, from the tiger in the *Calvin and Hobbes* cartoon), and he is short-haired. He also has purple/black spots on his tongue.

Hobbes's story is somewhat tragic. He and four siblings were abandoned by their mother when they were just a few weeks old. They were hand-fed by a volunteer working with the homeless animal rescue team, which allowed us to adopt Hobbes. Unfortunately, two of his siblings did not survive. The other two surviving siblings, both females, have found loving homes and are well cared for.

Figure ACT.3 Hobbes at 10 weeks old

Hobbes's temperament appears to include aspects of both Loki and Meika. He has a lot of energy, similar to Loki, which will hopefully dissipate somewhat with age. He also shows an adventurous spirit, again like Loki. Hobbes is very loving and loves to play or interact with humans, which is similar to both Meika and Loki. Nonetheless, Hobbes, like some people, can find it difficult to calm himself. Eventually, he is able to calm himself and then will either lie on the couch or beside my feet when we are at the office.

In 2011, Hobbes was not certified to provide AAT, but due to Meika's failing health, I needed to start bringing Hobbes to my office, as it was obvious that Meika was physically unable to manage two days a week. To do this, I needed to ask my clients if they would be willing to allow me to bring an uncertified dog into their therapy work. Fortunately, all of my clients agreed and provided their consent for Hobbes to start working with them before he was certified for AAT. After obtaining the clients' approval, Hobbes initially started working one day a week. As part of Hobbes's training, clients were asked to initially ignore him as they entered the room, as he was sure to rush to greet them and start licking whatever body part was available. They were also instructed to ask Hobbes to sit and give them his paw, thus engaging his brain and allowing his body to relax. Once he had sufficiently calmed himself, he could then be given permission to join the client on the sofa, receive some petting, or kiss the client, which is Hobbes's favorite thing to do. Hobbes is now working two days week, as Meika retired at the end of 2011. Hobbes passed his canine good citizen and therapy dog evaluations in 2012.

Last but not least is the newest addition to our family pack, Zoey, a Siberian husky–shepherd mix. At 12 weeks she has learned her name and how to respond to verbal and signal commands of "sit" and "lay." Again, Zoey is a rescue puppy that was taken to a kill shelter at 6-1/2 weeks of age with her five siblings. A local pet rescue agency took all six puppies and found them homes. We were lucky enough to find her. She has become a valued member of our family and is particular close to her brother, Hobbes, who we affectionately refer to as Zoey's favorite soft toy.

Figure ACT.4 Zoey at 12 weeks

Chapter
1

An Introduction to Animal-Assisted Psychotherapy

A young scared boy enters the therapist's office. He is wary and distrusting of adults; after all, they are the ones who have been hurting him. He doesn't know why he is there, just that he's been told to come see a "doctor of feelings." What does that mean, "feelings?" He's not allowed to have any feelings, just to be quiet and good, always good, which is so hard for him.

As he enters this stranger's room, feeling scared, suspicious, and wary, he sees a big dog walking towards him. The first thing he notices is that the dog is smiling and wagging his tail. The dog comes over to him, sniffs him, nudges the boy's hand with his nose, and then licks his hand as if it's the best thing in the world. Immediately, the boy senses the dog's acceptance of him; he

knows that this dog likes him no matter
what.

Suddenly the "feeling doctor"
speaks. The boy immediately thinks that he
is in trouble and moves away from the dog
toward the door, just in case. The woman
says, "Loki likes you. Would you like to get
to know Loki?" The boy nods
apprehensively; after all, this is the way it
always starts; they are nice at first, and then
he does something that makes them angry.
Why would she be any different from the
others, he thinks.

The therapist walks past the boy
and notices that he flinches, just a small
flinch, but she sees it. She sits in an
armchair and invites the boy to go to the
dog. He does, but he watches her closely. A
few minutes later, the boy is lost in play with
the dog; he barely notices the woman
anymore. The therapist watches the boy
and dog play, saying nothing. Sometime
later, the boy asks, "what kind of dog is it?"
The therapist explains that Loki is a collie
mix. The boy doesn't understand that, so
the counselor explains that Loki was
abandoned as a puppy at a shelter, and all
the people at the shelter could tell her was
that Loki was a collie and some other breed
of dog. The boy goes back to playing with
Loki, ignoring the therapist. A short while
later the time is up, and the therapist

indicates that it is time for the boy to say good-bye to Loki. He does and starts to leave. The therapist asks if he would like to come again to play with Loki or the counselor's other therapy dog, Meika. The boy smiles, almost imperceptibly, and hesitantly nods "yes." The therapist smiles and says that she is sure Loki or Meika would like to play with him again.

This interaction demonstrates part of the animal co-therapist's power: to allay the valid fears of a young life that has thus far been full of pain and uncertainty. The therapy dog brings some safety, acceptance, and love to the child, even if just for a few moments. The therapy dogs' power is in their unconditional acceptance of the human; and thus begins the work with animal-assisted psychotherapy (AAP).

My interest in AAP first began when I was in graduate school at the University of North Texas. One day when I was sitting in the psychology clinic's front office, I noticed one of my professors, Dr. Mahoney, entering the building accompanied by his small dog "Baby." As they entered the building, I noticed that people would stop and smile; heated conversations were halted, and people turned to greet the happy-go-lucky dog. Hardly anyone paid attention to Dr. Mahoney, only to Baby, who gladly visited with everyone and received some petting. Even one of the serious office workers who rarely smiled did so as Baby approached him, and he started talking to Baby in a childlike voice. I was intrigued by the phenomenon this little dog created just by her presence.

A short while after that experience, I took a course on psychotherapy. Part of the course requirements was to present a modality of therapy that was not presented by the instructor. We were also required to engage in a mock therapy scenario. Having witnessed the phenomenon that Baby had created, I became interested in whether dogs assist in therapy. So, I conducted research and discovered that dogs do indeed work alongside therapists in psychotherapy settings.

After presenting on AAP to my class cohorts and instructor, I then approached the instructor to ask if I could practice AAP in my mock therapy. The instructor agreed, and so I contacted the actor who would perform in my mock therapy sessions, and I contacted Dr. Mahoney to ask whether Baby might join the sessions. Everyone agreed.

The mock therapy scenario required that the actor come to eight weekly sessions to receive treatment for a designated mental illness. During the mock therapy, Baby would sometimes sit next to the "patient," me, or in the corner of the room. However, when the actor became tearful, Baby, who had been sitting by me, got up and walked across to the patient and started licking her hand. I commented on Baby's actions and inquired as to the patient's thoughts about them. The patient indicated that she felt comforted by Baby coming to her when she was upset. At the end of the mock therapy sessions, the actor was required to write her thoughts regarding the therapy. One of the actor's comments described how the patient felt loved and accepted by Baby, especially when she was upset.

Later, I discovered that at the University of North Texas, Dr. Cynthia Chandler directed the Center for Animal-Assisted Therapy. I contacted Dr. Chandler and inquired about courses that she instructed. She indicated that during the coming term, she was teaching a basic animal-assisted therapy (AAT) course. Of course, I signed up for this. Through the curriculum, I was introduced to the Delta Society and its volunteer program for animal-assisted therapy and activities (AATA). The course also allowed for an evaluation of a dog and me to see if we were suitable, both individually and as a team, for volunteering to provide AATA. I was delighted when Meika and I both passed the Delta Society's evaluation to become volunteers for AATA.

The next year, I obtained an American Psychological Association approved internship. My internship consisted of part-time work at two agencies. One was a local university's counseling center, and the other was a local nonprofit community services agency. After I started my internship, I approached the clinical director of the nonprofit community service agency and inquired whether they would allow me to utilize AAP during my internship. Of course, the clinical director had to determine if this was appropriate and then gain the approval of the executive director of the agency. One of the conditions of the approval was that I obtain supervision from someone skilled in AAP. I contacted Dr. Chandler again, and she agreed to supervise my work in AAP. The executive director of the agency reluctantly agreed, indicating that if any problems occurred, the use of AAP would be discontinued immediately.

Some of the vignettes in this book are from cases I worked on during my internship; others are from the private practice I started after obtaining my license as a clinical psychologist. At the end of the internship year, the nonprofit agency held a "good-bye party" for all of the interns and externs. During the gathering, the executive director of the agency stated to everyone that, although she had been hesitant to allow me to bring my therapy dogs to the agency, she was pleasantly surprised to see how the dogs' "presence" improved morale and boosted happiness for the staff, and she was amazed by the impact it had on my clients. She indicated that she would be more than happy to consider other therapists who wanted to use AAP as a modality in her agency.

Since that time, I have utilized AAP as a primary modality for therapy with my clients. I have also presented on AAP for mental health professional and non-mental health professional organizations. I am constantly amazed at what the therapy dogs bring to the process of therapy with clients. The journey has been amazing, a wonderful learning experience, and has provided therapeutic interventions that have proved successful and beneficial to my clients. Because of these experiences, I have decided to write this book.

The book's main purpose is to illustrate the therapy dogs' powerful effect on the psychotherapy process. The initial chapters, however, will help readers to

- Gain knowledge of the history of AAT;
- Distinguish between service dogs and therapy dogs;
- Distinguish between animal-assisted activities (AAA) and AAT;
- Understand the risks and benefits of AAP ;
- Know what type of dog is suitable to become a therapy dog;

- Comprehend the training the dog needs to be considered a therapy dog;
- Understand how to determine whether a therapy dog is becoming stressed by the work and how to manage the dog's stress; and
- Appreciate the many therapeutic roles a therapy dog provides.

The remainder of the book offers case vignettes illustrating how the therapy dogs assist in the therapy process. The vignettes use planned and unplanned interventions to demonstrate how the therapy dogs assist both the therapist and the client. The animal-assisted interventions are directed at decreasing clients' symptoms related to mental illness and/or improving their quality of life.

The vignettes presented are related to psychotherapy for children, adolescents, adults, families, and group psychotherapy, and the stories demonstrate the assistance that the furry facilitator provides to the human therapist. Clinical issues addressed in the vignettes include how the therapy dog assists in establishing the therapeutic relationship, allowing the client to accept touch, exploring incest, building self-esteem, mastery of frustration, becoming more aware of one's emotions, grounding, and other important clinical issues. Finally, this book includes a chapter in which previous clients provide reflections on their therapy with the therapy dogs.

It should be noted that names, dates, and places have been changed in the vignettes to protect the identities of the clients, and two clients have been synthesized in one of the vignettes. Moreover, in some cases I have referred to one of my furry facilitators when the actual case involved a different therapy dog; again, this is done to maintain confidentiality and to protect the clients' identities.

It is my hope that this book will provide readers with a broad understanding of the clinical application and power of AAP. If the reader is able to enjoy this book half as much as I have enjoyed my experience in this work and writing about it, then I will consider the book a huge success.

Chapter 2

What is A Therapy Dog and How Do We Define Animal-Assisted Psychotherapy?

I was recently contacted by someone who was calling on behalf of a friend. During the conversation, I asked, as I usually do, if this person and the friend knew that I am an animal-assisted therapist. The person replied that she had heard that I was an animal-assisted therapist but that she "hoped I would work with people too."

It is apparent from this brief vignette that people do not generally understand certain aspects of human-animal interactions and the roles beyond companions that animals play in people's lives. This chapter focuses on defining the various types of specially trained dogs that work with humans in numerous ways. It is important to understand the differences among these types of dogs and how therapy dogs are distinct, particularly given that other animal species can be similarly trained to work with humans.[1]

Definitions

What is a Therapy Dog and What is Not Considered a Therapy Dog?

It is important to distinguish the many ways in which dogs help humans. There are two main categories describing how dogs assist or facilitate human processes: The first is a "service dog," and the second is a "therapy dog." A service dog is not considered to be a pet according to the American with Disabilities Act (ADA), whereas a therapy dog may refer to a pet dog that has been trained to provide affection and comfort to people in hospitals, retirement homes, nursing homes, mental institutions, schools, and stressful situations such as disaster areas. Service dogs are trained to engage in specific behaviors related to the service they provide, such as detecting a seizure that is about to occur. Service dogs are trained by agencies, not owners, and are provided to people who need particular services.

Service dogs can be further sub-categorized into dogs that work with medical and mental health patients and dogs that work with police, fire, military, search and rescue,

---

[1] Chandler (2005, 2012); Fine (2010); Mills and Yeager (2012); Skloot (2009).

and U.S. Customs and Border Protection personnel. As the latter type of service dogs are not the focus of this book, they will not be discussed further, but I have provided resources related to them in Appendix A. I will, however, discuss medical and mental health service dogs to differentiate them from therapy dogs.

Medical/Mental Health Service Dogs

Medical and mental health service dogs are specifically trained to assist individuals with disabilities in different ways and thus fall under the domain of Title III of the Americans with Disabilities Act of 1990.[2] Section 36.104 of the ADA defines a service dog as follows:

> *Service animal* means any dog that is individually trained to do work or perform tasks for the benefit of an individual with a disability, including a physical, sensory, psychiatric, intellectual, or other mental disability. Other species of animals, whether wild or domestic, trained or untrained, are not service animals for the purposes of this definition. The work or tasks performed by a service animal must be directly related to the handler's disability. Examples of work or tasks include, but are not limited to,

---

[2] ADA, 42 U.S.C., 1281; Fine (2010); Matuszek (2010); Miller (2010); Mills and Yeager (2012); Shubert (2012a); Skloot (2009).

assisting individuals who are blind or have low vision with navigation and other tasks, alerting individuals who are deaf or hard of hearing to the presence of people or sounds, providing non-violent protection or rescue work, pulling a wheelchair, assisting an individual during a seizure, alerting individuals to the presence of allergens, retrieving items such as medicine or the telephone, providing physical support and assistance with balance and stability to individuals with mobility disabilities, and helping persons with psychiatric and neurological disabilities by preventing or interrupting impulsive or destructive behaviors. The crime deterrent effects of an animal's presence and the provision of emotional support, well-being, comfort, or companionship do not constitute work or tasks for the purposes of this definition.[3]

The followings list indicates the types of medical and mental health service dogs and their required activities:

1. Guide Dog: This service dog assists individuals with either full or partial vision loss.
2. Mobility Dog: This service dog can retrieve items, open doors, or even push buttons for its companion. This service animal can also assist

---

[3] ADA, 42 U.S.C., 1281, Section 36.104.

people with walking, balance, and transferring from place to place.

3. Signal or Hearing Alert Dog: This service dog alerts people with hearing loss to sounds.

4. Seizure Alert Dog/Seizure Response Dog: Also known as a medical alert dog, this service dog alerts people to oncoming seizures and is trained to respond to seizures with commands such as "get help" or to stay with the person until help arrives.

5. Medical Alert Dog/Medical Response Dog: This service dog is trained to alert to oncoming medical conditions, such as heart attack, stroke, diabetes, and epilepsy. These dogs can also be trained to assist with balance, movement, retrieving objects, turning lights on and off, calling an elevator, opening doors, and making 911 calls.

6. Autism Service Dog: This service dog can alert its companion to certain behaviors so that the person may keep these behaviors to a minimum. These dogs help people with autism to perform various daily activities, thus helping them to gain confidence and independence.

7. Psychiatric Service Dog: This service dog is individually trained to do work or perform tasks that mitigate a person's disability, such as panic attacks, dissociation, and symptoms of post-traumatic stress, including nightmares and flashbacks. The services may include providing environmental assessment (in such cases as paranoia or hallucinations), signaling behaviors

(such as interrupting repetitive or injurious behaviors), reminding the person to take medication, retrieving objects, guiding the human companion away from stressful situations, or acting as a brace if the person becomes unstable.[4] See Miller's book *Healing Companions* for more information about psychiatric service dogs.[5]

8. Service Dogs for Diabetics: This service dog is trained to identify minor scent changes created by hypoglycemia or low blood sugar and to take necessary steps, such as alerting medical response. These dogs are also trained to track the shifting levels of a person's condition and to alert the person to check blood sugar levels or to take necessary medications. These dogs detect faint changes in scent that cannot be detected by humans and, hence, prove to be worthy companions for people with diabetes.

Therapy Dogs

According to the ADA a therapy dog refers to a pet dog that is trained to provide affection and comfort to people in hospitals, retirement homes, nursing homes, mental institutions, schools, and stressful situations such as disaster areas. Therapy dogs provide animal contact to numerous

---

[4] Fine (2010); Miller (2010); Skloot (2009).
[5] Miller (2010)

individuals who might or might not have disabilities.[6] Therapy dogs are not considered service dogs and are not allowed, by federal law, access to public buildings.[7]

Figure 2.1 Loki at 10 Weeks

Animal-Assisted Psychotherapy

A therapy animal works in animal-assisted activities and/or animal-assisted therapy (AAA/AAT). The animal is usually the personal pet of a human companion and typically works with the companion during sessions. AAT involves including a pet as a "therapeutic agent."[8] This book mainly pertains to animal-assisted psychotherapy (AAP), which is the practice of allowing a trained therapy dog to assist in the psychotherapy process.

---

[6] ADA (1990); Beck et al. (2012); Butler (2004); Kinsley, Barker, and Barker (2012); Mills and Yeager (2012); Shubert (2012a); Watkins (2012).

[7] Butler (2004); Mills and Yeager (2012); Shubert (2012a).

[8] Chandler (2005, p. 2).

There are different roles for therapy dogs. Dogs can be trained and certified in the provision of AAA or AAT. The chart below outlines the distinction between these categories:

AAA	AAT
Casual "meet and greet" activities that involve pets visiting people.	Is a significant part of treatment for people who are physically, socially, emotionally, or cognitively challenged.
No specific treatment goals planned.	Stated goals for each session.
Same activity can be used with many people.	Individualized treatment plan for each patient.
Notes are unnecessary.	Notes on patient progress are made after each session, with revised goals or treatment plan, as needed.
Visit content is spontaneous.	Visit scheduled, usually at specified intervals, such as daily, biweekly, weekly, monthly, or some other prearranged interval.
Visit can be long or short.	Length of visit is pre-determined to best fit needs of patient.

Animal-assisted activities are considered a type of animal-assisted therapy activity. The major difference between AAA and AAT is that AAT involves health or human service workers or volunteers along with their certified therapy dogs in the usual practice of providing goal-directed interventions that are documented according to the workers' or volunteers' professional practice.[9] According to Yeager and Irwin, the office of the Surgeon General/Army Medical Command defines AAT as "the use of a certified animal to facilitate patient recovery from physical, mental, or social illness, using the pet as a 'co-therapist' to achieve a specific therapy goal."[10] The Delta Society indicates that specific mental health goals can include but are not limited to increasing attention, self-esteem, motivation, verbal communications, and reducing anxiety and loneliness.[11]

As you can see from the definitions on the previous pages, AAP easily falls under the guidelines related to AAT. As a therapist, I develop a treatment plan for each client I work with; we work on a goal in a session, and I keep notes on the sessions and the client's progress and will revise the goals or treatment plan if needed. Additionally, my clients' sessions are scheduled weekly or less often, depending on each client's progress in therapy. My sessions are typically 45, 60, or 75 minutes, again depending on the complexity

---

[9] Beck et al. (2012); Burch (1996); Chandler (2005); Delta Society (2000); Eggiman (2006); Fine (2010); Friesen (2010); Fike, Najera, and Dougherty (2012); Geist (2011); Grado (2011); King (2007); Lange, Cox, Bernert, and Jenkins (2006); Matuszek (2010); Mills and Yeager (2012); Minatrea and Wesley (2008); Peterson (1999); Parish-Plass (2008); Pichot (2012); Shubert (2012a & b); Souter and Miller (2007); Wilkes (2009).

[10] Yeager and Irwin (2012, pp. 59-60).

[11] The Delta Society (2000).

of the treatment plan and the client's goals. These criteria follow the criteria for AAT.

Animals in AAP form part of a triangle comprising the client, the therapist, and the therapeutic animal. Thus, it is important that anyone working in the modality of AAP understand the dynamics of this triangulation from the perspective of the therapist, the client, and the therapeutic animal.[12] The next several chapters explore this concept in detail.

---

[12] King (2007); Parish-Plass (2013); Walsh (2009).

Chapter
3

What is Animal-Assisted Psychotherapy?

A History of Animal-Assisted Psychotherapy

One of the first practices of animals in therapy was in ninth-century Belgium, in Gheel. Here, animals were considered a natural part of the therapy practiced to help rehabilitate "handicapped" individuals. In 1792 at the York Retreat in England, animals were part of the treatment of mentally ill patients. Most places were restraining and shackling patients, but the York Retreat's program promoted kindness, understanding, and reinforcement of self-control. Patients learned self-control in part by caring for rabbits and poultry. Nonetheless, this care of the animals did not involve pets as psychotherapeutic adjuncts.[1]

Later, in 1867, at an establishment for the treatment of epileptics in Germany, called Bethel, animals assisted in the therapeutic process. Here, small and large domestic animals as well as farm animals participated.[2]

Some authors report that the U.S. military first promoted the assistance of dogs in therapeutic interventions for psychiatric patients in 1919 at St. Elizabeth's Hospital in Washington, D.C. Later, in 1940, at the Pawling Army Air Force Convalescent Center in Pawling, New York animals were also included as part of the therapeutic process. It is also reported that in 1985, the U.S. Army Veterinary Corps started to develop a better understanding of the human-animal connection and its possible benefits for humans. This led to the establishment of the U.S. Army Service Dog Training Center (STDC) in 1995, at Fort Knox, to assist physically disabled veterans and their families. Since then, the military have developed numerous programs related to AAT at several military centers. In one of these programs, injured service personnel train military service dogs for other injured military personnel.[3]

According to some authors, Sigmund Freud judged human personality with the assistance of his chow dog, Jo-

---

[1] Burch (1996); Delta Society (2000); Eggiman (2006); Fine (2010); Marr et al. (2000); Matuszek (2010; Parshall (2003); Pichot (2012); Sacks (2008); Shubert (2012a & b); Reichert (1998).

[2] Butler (2004; Delta Society (2000); Fine (2010); Marr et al. (2000); Matuszek (2010); Parshall (2003); Reichert (1998); Shubert (2012b); Wilkes (2009).

[3] Burch (1990); Beck et al. (2012); Chandler (2012); Chumley (2012); Matuszek (2010); Shubert (2012a).

Fi. Therefore, Jo-Fi attended all of Freud's sessions with patients. Freud also reportedly could identify the amount of tension his patients were experiencing by the position in which Jo-Fi lay in relation to a patient, such that when Jo-Fi lay close to a patient, Freud believed that this meant the patient had no tension. Freud understood that dogs are generally unmoved by what patients say, and therefore, the dog provided a sense of safety, remained calm, and appeared to accept his patients' embarrassing and painful declarations. Freud also believed that his patients' resistance appeared to diminish when his dog was present. These factors appear to demonstrate what Winnicott called the "holding environment." The holding environment consists of the therapist and/or co-therapist creating a safe environment that is supportive, questioning, and provides empathy, a voice laden with compassion, a sense of steadiness in the therapist or co-therapist, and a belief that the therapist will be there and can tolerate what is being shared.[4]

According to one author, however, the therapeutic use of animals first occurred in the United States in the 1940s at the convalescent home for the Air Force and involved the observation, care, and touching of animals to promote patients' well-being.[5]

Rubenstein and Watkins indicate that AAT has been utilized by the military since World War I and that the U.S. Army began to investigate the positive benefits of the human-animal connection in the 1960s.[6] According to

---

[4] Eggiman (2006); Fine (2010); Moore and Fine (1990); Pichot (2012); Sacks (2008); Shubert (2012b); Walsh (2009); Wilkes (2009).

[5] Parshall (2003).

[6] Rubenstein (2012); Watkins (2012).

Conrad, a stray dog, later named "Stubby," wandered into the 102nd infantry camp and befriended soldiers, and when the division was sent to France, "STUBBY did his part by providing morale-lifting visits up and down the line and occasional early warning about gas attacks or by waking a sleeping sentry to alert him to a German attack."[7]

Figure 3.1 Sgt. Stubby
Photo obtained at
http://en.wikipedia.org/wiki/Sergeant_Stubby

Also according to Conrad, "Dogs were formally used during World War II, Korea and Vietnam in such roles as guards, and patrolling scouts, but whether the dog is employed in a formal program or not you can be sure that wherever there are soldiers in need of comfort and companionship there will always be a faithful dog nearby."[8] Although these dogs might have been considered "service

---

[7] Conrad (1998).
[8] Conrad (1998).

dogs," it appears that they might have played two roles, that of a service dog and a therapy dog.

Figure 3.2 Military Dogs

Other authors report that therapy dogs have been sent into war areas, such as Iraq and Afghanistan, as part of specific programs aimed at reducing stress for military personnel, and the presence of the dogs appeared to promote attendance at stress and anxiety classes, possibly by reducing the stigma of needing such help. These authors further indicate that human-animal bond programs have been implemented at both the Walter Reed Army Medical Center and the Walter Reed Army National Medical Center. Moreover, therapy dogs provide physical and emotional support to veterans and are used to aid in the treatment of post-traumatic stress disorder (PTSD) and other mental illnesses.[9]

---

[9] Chumley (2012); Fike, Najera, and Dougherty (2012); Foreman and Crosson (2012); Ritchie and Amaker (2012); Rubenstein (2012); Yeager and Irwin (2012); Yount, Olmert, and Lee (2012).

According to Chandler as well as Golin and Walsh, Green Chimneys Children's Services in Brewster, New York, has been utilizing AAT since 1948, particularly to foster caring between animals and children, for the children to learn that they too can be cared for, and to help the children "open up."[10]

Later, in 1953 in the United States, Dr. Boris Levinson inadvertently introduced his dog Jingles into the therapeutic process and noticed the therapeutic implication. A problem child who had been unsuccessfully treated was referred to Levinson. When the parent and child arrived an hour before their appointment, Jingles ran to the child and licked him. Until this point, the child had been withdrawn and uncommunicative. The child cuddled with Jingles and petted him, asking if the dog played with other children. When Dr. Levinson stated that Jingles played with children, the boy asked if he could come back again and play with Jingles. For the next few sessions, the boy was allowed to play with Jingles while Dr. Levinson observed. Eventually, the boy asked Dr. Levinson to join their play, which led to the establishment of a good working relationship and the successful treatment of the boy.[11]

From this work, Levinson formulated and developed in 1984 the four ways a therapist can allow a dog to assist in the therapeutic process: 1) as a

---

[10] Chandler (2012); Golin and Walsh (1994).

[11] Berry, Borgi, Francia, Alleva, and Cirulli (2012); Burch (1996); Butler (2004); Chandler (2005, 2012); Chumley (2012); Eggiman (2006); Fine (2010); Friesen (2010); Geist (2011); Grado (2011); King (2007); Lange et al. (2006); Levinson (1962, 1997); Matuszek (2010); Parshall (2003); Pitts (2005); Reichert (1998); Sacks (2008); Shubert (2012a & b); Walsh (2009); Wilkes (2009); Zilcha-Mano, Mikulincer, and Shaver (2011).

psychotherapeutic adjunct; 2) sole therapist; 3) as a catalyst for change; and 4) as a means of contact with nature. This book focuses on pets and animals as an adjunct, accessory, tool, and technique in the therapeutic process.

According to Chandler and Shubert, Elizabeth and Sam Corson expanded on Levinson's work by integrating animals into hospitals and nursing homes, and they noted improvement in many areas, including psychological issues.[12] The introduction of therapy dogs into the treatment of psychiatric patients who had been difficult to treat led to improvements in staff-patient and patient-patient interactions and relationships.

In 1976, Elaine Smith formed Therapy Dogs International, and in 1977, Leo Bustad formed the Delta Foundation, now known as Pet Partners and formerly known as the Delta Society. These two agencies were developed to assess human-animal teams that could be considered suitable for providing AAA and AAT. Therapy Dogs International and Pet Partners' main role related to AAT is to certify both people and dogs as having the appropriate training and grounding to perform the work of AAA and AAT. Other certification agencies for AAA and/or AAT include the American Kennel Club and Therapy Dogs International. [13]

Several authors state that therapy dogs have assisted the military both in combat areas and in medical centers since 1992. Initially, the dogs were part of "Combat and Operational Stress Control" teams, which provided

---

[12] Chandler (2005, 2012); Shubert (2012a).

[13] Burch (1996); Chandler (2005, 2012); Chumley (2012); Delta Society (2000); Eggiman (2006); Fine (2010); Lange et al. (2006); Parshall (2003); Sacks (2008); Shubert (2012a & b); Wilkes (2009).

education and therapy in places of war. These teams were designed and implemented to help prevent or ameliorate stress and to reduce the stigma of seeking behavioral/mental health care. Later, two therapy dogs were sent to Iraq in 2007 to provide stress relief unparalleled by people.[14]

Figure 3.3 Military Dogs Parachuting

Several authors further state that the army is attempting to optimize the dogs that participate in combat and in stress-reduction and other programs involving "Wounded Warriors" and veterans returning to civilian life; the army is also attempting to clarify the difference between service dogs and therapy dogs.[15]

---

[14] Beck et al. (2012); Chumley (2012); Fike, Najera, and Dougherty (2012); Gregg (2012); Krol (2012); Ritchie and Amaker (2012); Watkins (2012); Yeager and Irwin (2012).

[15] Beck et al. (2012); Chumley (2012); Mills and Yeager (2012); Watkins (2012); Yeager and Irwin (2012).

According to Shubert, therapy dogs first assisted in a major disaster/crisis response in 1995 for the bombing of the Murrah Building in Oklahoma City, and later, in 1998, for a shooting at Thurston High School in Springfield, Oregon.[16] The main purpose of the therapy dogs was to provide comfort and support directly after these disasters. Later, therapy dogs assisted police, fire, and rescue personnel in New York City after the terrorist attacks of September 11, 2001.

In 2008, Yount, Olmert, and Lee created a program designed to help ameliorate symptoms of PTSD in veterans.[17] The program they developed is now offered through a non-profit foundation called Warrior Canine Connection, and it has provided anecdotal evidence that a veteran trainer's symptoms of PTSD are reduced as a result of training the therapy dogs. Yount, Olmert, and Lee report that the Warrior Canine Connection program, which is based on shaping positive behaviors in the service dog, helps the trainers to master their own emotions, to improve their ability to maintain attention, to improve social skills, and to obtain a better sense of well-being.[18] They further state that some benefits flow beyond the warrior-canine connection to others who interact with them in the medical setting, such as health care workers and other patients. Moreover, according to Yount, Olmert, and Lee, clinicians reported that the warrior trainers demonstrated improvements in several areas:

---

[16] Shubert (2012b).

[17] Yount, Olmert, and Lee (2012).

[18] Ibid.

- Impulse control ;
- Emotional regulation and/or emotional display;
- Reduced numbness;
- Sleep;
- Depressive symptoms;
- Decrease in startle responses;
- Sense of connection to others; and
- Decreased use of medications.[19]

Figure 3.4 Military Dog Providing AAT

Currently, there are numerous agencies that provide some form of AAA, AAT, or AAP. Some of these agencies include Companions for Heroes, Pets2Vets, Specialized Therapy K-9 Programs, Canines for Combat Veterans, the

---

[19] Ibid.

Warrior Service Dog Training Program, Dog Tags, Canine Companions for Independence, the Prison PUP Program, and others.[20]

Others have also studied and written about AAT, such as Parshall, who reported on two studies, one in the United States and one in Australia, which found that owning a pet is beneficial to the cardiac health of the human owner.[21] Parshall further reported that these studies also found benefits related to lowering blood pressure. In other studies, Parshall indicates that animals act as a stress buffer, provide social support, that patients tend to open up more when an animal is present, and that therapy animals generally have a positive impact on the physical and mental health of human patients.[22]

Grado indicates that AAP can help teach respect and responsibility to patients in that mental health providers will likely instruct their patients on how to approach a therapy dog and how to behave with the dog.[23] Grado also reports that these social skills might then generalize to others.[24] Finally, Grado and Lind state that AAT programs can help children practice life skills, promote motivation, improve self-esteem, and help build skills for social interaction.[25]

According to Friesen, therapy dogs have contributed to elementary-age children's emotional

---

[20] Alers and Simpson (2012); Fine (2010); Foreman and Crosson (2012); Miller (2010); Yeager and Irwin (2012).

[21] Parshall (2003).

[22] Ibid.

[23] Grado (2011).

[24] Ibid.

[25] Grado (2011); Lind (2009).

stability, and for children diagnosed with severe emotional disorders, the dogs have helped the children to develop a positive attitude towards school.[26] Like other researchers, Friesen indicates that AAP has helped school-aged children to increase their self-esteem and be more attentive, responsive, and cooperative.[27] Moreover, she indicates that in a therapeutic setting, children involved in AAP demonstrated increased alertness and attention span, enhanced openness, and desire for social contact. Finally, Friesen reports that "children's interactions with therapy dogs include the acceptance and non-judgmental bond," which helps to improve relationships with peers and adults. She further suggests that this can occur in one of three ways: 1) The therapy dog appears to provide unconditional social support for children by acting as a "friend;" 2) the therapy dog's spontaneous eagerness for interaction possibly provides stimulus for the child's own social behaviors; and 3) the therapy dog appears to increase positive interactions.[28]

Many authors have reported the benefits of the Reading Education Assistance Dogs (R.E.A.D ©) program for children with reading difficulties. The R.E.A.D. program was started in 1995 in Salt Lake City. According to the research conducted by the R.E.A.D. program and others, students utilizing the R.E.A.D. program can increase their reading skill by two grade levels. These authors claim that the presence of the dog motivates the

---

[26] Friesen (2010), p 262.
[27] Ibid.
[28] Friesen (2010).

children to read, and they do not feel judged by their canine companion should they make a reading mistake.[29]

Figure 3.5 A "Reading Dog"

According to Sacks, since the late 1990s many scholars have researched the benefits of AAP, and she reports that the researchers determined the following: "The researchers distinguished the importance of the animal not being the therapist, but having acted as a *prosthesis* facilitating the establishment of a therapeutic relationship by the therapist."[30]

Since then, numerous articles have been published in magazines, newspapers, and journals, including many research articles on the benefits of AAP.[31]

---

[29] Chandler (2005, 2012); Eggiman (2006); Fine (2010); Friesen (2010); Grado (2011); Jalongo (2005); Jalongo, Astorino, and Bomboy (2004); King (2007).

[30] Sacks (2008, p. 504).

[31] Berry et al. (2012); Chandler, Portrie-Bethke, Barrio Minton, Fernando, and O'Callaghan (2010); Friesen (2010); Grado (2011); Johnson (2011); King (2007); Kinsley, Barker, and Barker (2012); Krol (2012); Marr et al. (2000); Mills and Yeager (2012); Prothmann et al. (2005); Schultz, Remick-Barlow, and Robbins (2007); Souter and Miller (2007); Zilcha-Mano, Mikulincer, and Shaver (2011).

Description of Animal-Assisted Psychotherapy

AAP consists of a trained, licensed human therapist and a furry facilitator collaborating to assist in the recovery of someone receiving mental health services. AAP can include but is not limited to recovery from child abuse including physical, emotional, or sexual abuse, anxiety, depression, schizophrenia, pervasive developmental disorders, post-traumatic stress disorder, and deficiencies in social skills.

AAP consists of a specific treatment plan for the particular issues presented by the client, which includes the therapy dog facilitating the therapeutic process. The therapist can intentionally direct the therapy dog to help facilitate recovery, or the dog's assistance can occur without the therapist's direction but still be beneficial to the client.[32]

According to several authors, AAP facilitates therapy and can improve communication, enhance trust, motivate clients, and lead to a decrease in their stress and anxiety levels.[33]

---

[32] Berry et al. (2012); Chandler et al. (2010); Eggiman (2006); Geist (2011); Hanselman (2001); Jalongo (2005); Kinsley, Barker, and Barker (2012); Lange et al. (2006); Miller (2010); Mills and Yeager (2012); Minatrea and Wesley (2008); Peterson (1999); Prothmann, Bienert, and Ettrich (2006); Sacks (2008); Schultz, Remick-Barlow, and Robbins (2007); Shubert (2012b); Souter and Miller (2007); University of British Columbia, Okanagan (2012); Yeager and Irwin (2012); Yount, Olmert, and Lee (2012); Walsh (2009).

[33] Fike, Najera, and Dougherty (2012); King (2007); Minatrea and Wesley (2008); Peterson (1999); Pichot (2012); Yeager and Irwin (2012).

Chandler indicates that trained mental health professionals can use AAP, regardless of their theoretical orientation or the techniques that they use.[34] In my own experience as an animal-assisted therapist, I have observed that clients become more expressive, insightful, and trusting when my therapy dogs are present. In many cases, my clients have also noted this, and they report that because of the therapy dogs' presence, they feel safer, more easily comforted, and more trusting of me. I have also noted on numerous occasions that when clients are experiencing and processing difficult experiences, they will often reach out and pet the therapy dog, which appears to indicate that the therapy dogs are surrogates for a therapeutic touch that people seek in order to be comforted and that the human therapist might be unable to provide.

O'Callaghan and Chandler report that other researchers have indicated that AAP involves animal-assisted interventions (AAIs), which have been defined as any intentional or unintentional intervention that incorporates a therapeutic animal into the therapy process.[35] These and many other authors further state that researchers have found that the AAIs are therapeutically beneficial to those experiencing depression and anxiety, increase positive social interactions, decrease behavioral problems, and improve psychophysiological healing and health. [36]

---

[34] Chandler (2005, 2012).

[35] O'Callaghan and Chandler (2011).

[36] Beck et al. (2012); Berry et al. (2012); Chandler (2005, 2012); Chandler et al. (2010); Eggiman (2006); Fine (2010); Friesen (2010); Geist (2011); Golin and Walsh (1994); Gregg (2012); Hanselman (2001); Johnson (2011); King (2007); Kinsley, Barker, and Barker (2012); Lange et al. (2006); O'Callaghan and Chandler (2011); Marr et al. (2000); Miller (2010); Mills and Yeager (2012); Parshall (2003); Pichot

Some researchers have identified two aspects of AAP.[37] They define the first aspect as the animal-assisted therapy technique (AATT) and the second as the animal-assisted therapy intervention (AATI). The AATT involves the specific interventions utilized by a mental health professional in AAP. O'Callaghan and Chandler determined from literature reviews numerous AATTs and reported 18 specific techniques.[38] These include but are not necessarily limited to the following:

1. The counselor comments on the client-therapy dog's relationship;
2. The counselor encourages the client to play with the therapy dog in the session;
3. The counselor engages the therapy dog in performing tricks;
4. The counselor encourages the client to touch and/or pet the therapy dog;
5. The counselor encourages the client to express distress and concerns to the therapy dog;
6. The counselor encourages the client to engage the therapy dog in performing tricks;
7. The counselor develops specific activities that involve the therapy dog;

(2012); Prothmann et al. (2005); Sacks (2008); Schultz, Remick-Barlow, and Robbins (2007); Shubert (2012a); Souter and Miller (2007); Walsh (2009); University of British Columbia, Okanagan (2012); Yount, Olmert, and Lee (2012); Walsh (2009); Wilkes (2009).

[37] Chandler (2010); O'Callaghan and Chandler (2011).

[38] O'Callaghan and Chandler (2011).

8. The counselor allows the therapy dog to engage spontaneously with the client, and this is used in a therapeutic way;

9. The client, the therapy dog, and the counselor engage outside of the traditional therapy environment, such as taking a walk;

10. The counselor asks the client to command the therapy dog in some manner;

11. The counselor encourages the client to make up stories involving the therapy dog;

12. The counselor asks questions based on the client-therapy dog relationship; for example, "if Loki was your best friend, what would he know about you that no one else would know?";

13. The presence of a therapy dog;

14. Spontaneous interaction between the client and therapy dog is reflected by the counselor;

15. The use of animal stories or metaphors;

16. The counselor requests that the client recreate or reenact a specific role that the therapy dog has played;

17. The counselor shares with the client specific history about the therapy dog's family history; and

18. The counselor shares with the client other history related to the therapy dog.

These techniques or interventions are utilized in AAP, according to the researchers, to build rapport in the therapeutic relationship, to facilitate insight, to enhance the client's relationship skills, to improve the client's confidence, to enhance the client's social skills, to model specific behaviors, as a behavioral reward for the client, to enhance trust in the therapeutic environment, to encourage feelings to be shared, and to promote the feeling of safety in the therapeutic environment.[39]

---

[39] Chandler (2012); O'Callaghan and Chandler (2011).

Chapter

4

Where, with Whom, and How can Animal-Assisted Psychotherapy be Utilized?

Where can Animal-Assisted Psychotherapy be Provided?

Animal-assisted psychotherapy (AAP) can be provided in many different places, such as outpatient facilities, private practice, inpatient or residential treatment centers, hospitals, schools, hospices, prisons, shelters, and crisis intervention facilities.[1]

---

[1] Butler (2004); Eggiman (2006); Friesen (2010); Golin and Walsh (1994); Grado (2011); Jalongo, Astorino, and Bomboy (2004); Johnson (2011); King (2007); Lange et al. (2006); Marr et al. (2000); Mills and Yeager (2012); Minatrea and Wesley (2008); Peterson (1999); Pichot (2012); Prothmann, Bienert, and Ettrich (2006); Rubenstein (2012); Sacks (2008); Shubert (2012a & b); Souter and Miller (2007).

Patient Suitability

Generally, AAP is suitable for all ages, ethnicities, most cultural backgrounds, and both genders.[2] Marr et al. suggest that AAP can be helpful for children and adolescents with various diagnoses as well as adults.[3]

Nonetheless, before beginning to work with an individual in AAP, it is important to assess the suitability and acceptance of the person for this modality of treatment. Hence, before the first session occurs, it is important to discuss the person's feelings and attitudes towards animals, particularly dogs. What are the client's concerns and fears? Obviously, if s/he has an intense fear of animals or dogs, then a dog assisting as a therapeutic tool is not a good idea, but perhaps systematic desensitization can occur later. If the person has hurt animals or has been extremely violent toward humans in the past, this individual might not be suitable for AAP.[4]

Chandler states that if an animal similar to the therapy animal has previously hurt or injured the client in some way, then the person might not wish to engage in AAP.[5] This needs to be addressed before the potential client comes to the first session. Chandler suggests that in this

---

[2] Chandler (2005, 2012); Fine (2010); Geist (2011); Johnson (2011); King (2007); Lange et al. (2006); Lefkowitz et al. (2005); Minatrea and Wesley (2008); O'Callaghan and Chandler (2011); Parish-Plass (2008); Sacks (2008); Shubert (2012a & b; Zamir (2006).

[3] Marr et al. (2000).

[4] Chandler (2005, 2012); Fine (2010; Lefkowitz et al. (2005); Parshall (2003); Walsh (2009).

[5] Chandler (2005).

case, the therapy animal should not be introduced into the therapy process until the client asks for or agrees to the animal's presence.[6] Nonetheless, as in my case, when a therapist encounters a client who does not wish to have a therapy animal in the sessions, the therapist may wish or need to refer the person to someone else. In my particular situation, I do not have a safe place in my office, other than my office, where I can leave my therapy dog while I see clients. Therefore, I refer such clients to another counselor.

Finally, if a client has strong allergies to therapy dogs, s/he might not be a good candidate for AAP.[7] Nonetheless, Friesen indicates that only a small percentage of those seen by allergists (roughly 6%) demonstrate allergies to pet dander.[8] She also recommends that an animal that has limited shedding, is bathed and brushed regularly, is vaccinated, and is treated with an anti-allergen powder before engaging in AAP will likely help to reduce dander and minimize potential allergies. O'Callaghan and Chandler agree that when a client is allergic to animals, this is a good reason for not including the therapy dog in treatment.[9] Another reason they identify for not having a therapy dog in a session is impulse control issues in a client, which could lead the client to harm the therapy dog.

The Delta Society also agrees that AAP might not be appropriate for people with allergic reactions to dogs, people who have zoonotic diseases (see Chapter 5 for a more detailed explanation of this concern), people who are

---

[6] Ibid.

[7] Lefkowitz et al. (2005); Minatrea and Wesley (2008); Matuszek (2010); Walsh (2009).

[8] Friesen (2010).

[9] O'Callaghan and Chandler (2011).

extremely fearful of animals, individuals with a cultural background that indicates their view of animals would not be helpful, and individuals with brain injuries, developmental disabilities, and senility.[10]

What Can Animal-Assisted Psychotherapy Assist in Treating?

According to many authors, the modality of animal-assisted psychotherapy (AAP) can aid in the treatment of numerous different mental illnesses, such as depression, anxiety disorders, substance abuse, post-traumatic stress disorder, attachment disorder, autism spectrum disorders, and conduct disorder.[11]

Chandler indicates that AAP can be beneficial for working with clients who have been discouraged, unmotivated, ambivalent, disobedient, and who have poor insight, deficits in social skills, or barriers to developing healthy relationships.[12] King further indicates that AAP can be helpful in treating issues related to loneliness, abuse and neglect, self-esteem and self-worth, grief, interpersonal

---

[10] The Delta Society (2000).

[11] Chandler (2005, 2012); Eggiman (2006); Fine (2010); Geist (2011); Golin and Walsh (1994); Jalongo (2005); Johnson (2011); King (2007); Minatrea and Wesley (2008); O'Callaghan and Chandler (2011); Parish-Plass (2008); Pichot (2012); Reichert (1998); Sacks (2008); Schultz, Remick-Barlow, and Robbins (2007); Shubert (2012a); Souter and Miller (2007); Yeager and Irwin (2012; Yount, Olmert, and Lee (2012); Zamir (2006); Zilcha-Mano, Mikulincer, and Shaver (2011).

[12] Chandler (2005, 2012).

relationships, and appropriate touching.[13] Fine also posits that therapy dogs can provide therapeutic touch to a survivor of childhood abuse, whereas human therapists, given their professional training, might not feel it is appropriate for them to touch the client.[14]

Animal-Assisted Psychotherapy: A Session Format

Whether counselors work with individuals, couples, families, or groups, AAP is a useful tool. Whether therapists prefer a directive or a non-directive style, AAP can help the therapy process.[15] In my practice, I work with individuals, couples, families, and groups. I can also be directive and non-directive, and AAP helps with these processes.

Successful incorporation of AAP involves assessing how animal-assisted interventions can meet a client's needs, developing appropriate treatment goals that integrate animal-assisted interventions, and ensuring that therapists have sufficient knowledge and skill in applying animal-assisted interventions. The practice of AAP also requires that therapists continually assess the efficacy of the animal-assisted interventions, make adaptations if necessary, and stay up-to-date with research on AAP.[16]

---

[13] King (2007).
[14] Fine (2010).
[15] Chandler (2005).
[16] Chandler (2012).

Figure 4.1 Meika and Loki playing

In a typical session the therapy dog waits in my office while I walk the short 15 feet to the patient waiting area to escort the client back. The therapy dog is usually relaxing on a blanket, on the couch, or on the floor. When we return to the room, I always allow the client to enter the room first. Typically, upon entering the room, the therapy dog immediately gets up to greet the client. The therapy dog will wag his/her tail, come over to the client, and then follow the client back to wherever the client chooses to sit. Many but not all clients will spend several minutes saying "hello" to the therapy dog. Saying "hello" typically consists of clients petting and in some cases talking to the therapy dog, such as saying "hi" and asking how the dog is doing. After several moments of this interaction and typically when there is a natural break in these behaviors, I will then acknowledge clients verbally and check in with them. At this time, the therapy dog will either jump up on the couch beside the client, lie at the client's feet, come lie at my feet, or find another comfortable place in the room. Therapy then proceeds as is typical for most sessions.

In some cases, when clients are processing difficult affect, they might call the therapy dog to them and encourage the dog to sit on the couch beside them so that they may pet the dog to help relieve their tension. At other times, I might be more directive in asking the dog to be more engaged in the therapy process, such as performing a trick, asking the dog to sit with the client, having the dog become a grounding tool by asking the client to pet the dog, or in some cases the dog will spontaneously come over to the client, jump up on the couch, and either paw, nudge, or lick the person. If, during the session, the client says something particular about the therapy dog, I will typically inquire about the comment. Clients' comments about the therapy dog can include noticing that the therapy dog is dreaming, in which case I might ask them what they think the dog is dreaming about. In other cases, a client might state that s/he thinks the therapy dog is sad, in which case I will ask what it is about the dog that indicates this.

When the session is over, most clients will typically pet the therapy dog's head and say "good-bye." As they leave my therapy room, some clients might pat or rub a wooden sculpture of my retired therapy dog, Meika. In some cases, the client might ask how Meika is now doing, which I of course answer appropriately.

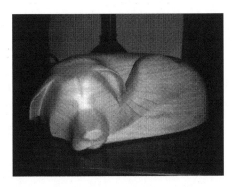

Figure 4.2 Wooden Sculpture of Meika

As you can see from the above description, the therapy dog might not be central to the therapy process. When engaged in the therapy process, however, the dog can be helpful in bringing to light the client's inner processes and emotional states, as many of the vignettes in the following chapters demonstrate.

A reasonable question regarding therapy sessions concerns whether the mental health professional should pet the therapy dog in a session? Chandler indicates that we should as this can demonstrate a nurturing, trusting, and positive relationship between the therapist and the therapy dog.[17] She also states that this interaction can encourage the client to pet the therapy dog.

When I first brought Hobbes to work, we were working on having him understand that I would provide petting on my terms, not when he nudged me to seek petting. I wanted Hobbes to understand that if he wanted attention, he was to seek it by coming and sitting by me and not by nudging me with his nose. In a group therapy session, for example, Hobbes came over to me and nudged me with his nose. I ignored him and thought no more of it. A few days later I met individually with a client who was in the group. She expressed her sadness in seeing me ignore Hobbes. She indicated that this was a "trigger" for her as her mother often ignored her needs and that seeing me ignore Hobbes led her to think that I was like her mother. After processing this situation further so that the client worked through this significant issue for her, I later explained that Hobbes is still learning his roles and

---

[17] Chandler (2005).

boundaries and that should she see this behavior again, I hoped that she could understand that I am still teaching him. Nonetheless, this situation does bring to light that in some cases, our clients are keenly attuned to the relationship between the therapist and the therapy dog and that in these cases, we can be important role models for our clients to model healthy adaptive relationships.

Regarding group therapy, Chandler describes how the therapy dog's interaction with the group members can demonstrate the group's unity and the role development of the group members.[18] As I have seen in my own groups, she reports that competition for the therapy dog's attention can occur, and whereas some members might ignore the therapy dog, others might pay the dog a lot of attention. I have also noted that some members prefer one therapy dog to another and that behavior or preference can be a topic of therapeutic discussion.

---

[18] Chandler (2005).

Chapter
5

What are the Benefits and Risks of Animal-Assisted Psychotherapy?

A man sits on the therapy sofa, leaning on his left side. Hobbes, the therapy dog, sits at the other end of the couch. The man is exploring how to tell his wife that he fears their relationship is getting worse and that she will leave him. As he speaks, he starts to tear up and attempts to choke back his feelings. At the same time, he slowly sits up and leans to his right. Reaching out his hand, he finds a furry facilitator, Hobbes. As he pets Hobbes, Hobbes moves towards the man and lays his head in the man's lap. Prompted by me, the man continues to explore his fear and loneliness, but now there is no choking back his feelings, just soft tears falling. As he continues to pet Hobbes, his tears subside, and he makes a plan to talk to his wife that weekend.

The simple benefit of comfort and support provided by the furry facilitator helps to alleviate the distress the man experiences and, with my assistance, allows him to process his fears and determine a plan to see if his fears are based in reality. Although this process could have been achieved without the therapy dog, I believe the therapy dog helps by providing some comfort to the man, which allows him to access his true thoughts and feelings. The man reaches out for comfort and finds it in the therapy dog. He cannot reach out to me like that because he understands the therapy rule that therapists do not touch clients in that way.

Benefits of Animal-Assisted Psychotherapy

Potential Benefits to the Therapy Process

I believe, as do others, that dogs acting as co-therapists enhance therapy in many different ways, mainly because the dogs change the process of therapy merely by being present and/or by engaging in specific behaviors. Therapy dogs act and therefore enhance the therapy process when they act as an ice-breaker, help build rapport, help to foster trust, are a source of comfort, accept unconditionally, fail to judge, and many other features as mentioned above and subsequently in this book. Others who share my beliefs have reported in numerous journals, articles, and books their study findings or anecdotal evidence regarding how therapy dogs enhance the process of therapy.[1] Later in this book, I describe specific examples of how AAP is beneficial to the therapy process and to my clients in particular.

Chandler describes how the therapy animal can bring "entertainment" to the therapy process by engaging in a trick or behaving in a comedic way.[2] This behavior can help break the ice or break clients' tension as well as lift them out of distressing emotions so that they can understand that feelings can change and might not be overwhelming, as some clients tend to believe. Therapy dogs can also promote clients' ability to modulate their emotions; this is especially true for those with borderline tendencies, which then allows such clients to use the rational part of the brain, instead of using only the emotional part of the brain. This can lead to the use of the "wise mind," the overlap of the rational and emotional parts of the brain.

The therapy process is also enhanced when the therapy dog can help the client to learn a skill, such as how to prevent or minimize a panic attack. In this case, when clients report that they are starting to notice sensations of a panic attack or anxiety, they are encouraged to place their

---

[1] Blum Barish (2002); Chandler (2005, 2012); Eggiman (2006); Fine (2010); Foreman and Crosson (2012); Friesen (2010); Geist (2011); Golin and Walsh (1994); Jalongo, Astorino, and Bomboy (2004); King (2007); Krol (2012); Johnson (2011); Perry, Rubinstein, and Austin (2012); Prothmann, Bienert, and Ettrich (2006); Reichert (1998); Rovner (2012); Walsh (2009); Wilkes (2009).

[2] Chandler (2005, 2012).

hand on the belly of the "furry facilitator," and as long as the furry facilitator is calm, clients are then asked to match their breathing to that of the slow, deep breathing of the therapy dog lying beside them. Clients can safely touch the furry facilitator, something that is discouraged with the human therapist, and start to breathe slowly and deeply, thus minimizing or preventing a panic attack from occurring. When this activity is repeated several times over several sessions, the client can internalize the process or imagine and use it later. See Chapter 13 for more details on this technique.

Potential Benefits for the Human Client

Many writers and researchers have reported the physiological benefits that occur when humans relate to an animal, including therapy dogs. These physiological benefits include decreased heart rate, decreased blood pressure, a more relaxed body posture, and a reduction in physical symptoms of anxiety.[3]

Another physiological benefit ascribed to therapy dogs and companion dogs is the release of oxytocin, a

---

[3] Beck et al. (2012); Berry et al. (2012); Chandler (2005, 2012); Chumley (2012); Eggiman (2006); Fine (2010); Friesen (2010); Geist (2011); Grado (2011); Jalongo (2005); Jalongo, Astorino, and Bomboy (2004); Johnson (2011); King (2007); Kinsley, Barker, and Barker (2012); Lange et al. (2006); Matuszek (2010); Minatrea and Wesley (2008); O'Callaghan & Chandler (2011); Parshall (2003); Pichot (2012); Peterson (1999); Rovner (2012); Souter and Miller (2007); Yeager and Irwin (2012); Yount, Olmert, and Lee (2012); Walsh (2009); Wilkes (2009).

hormone that helps us feel happy and connected. Research indicates higher levels of oxytocin in those engaging in AAP, and this therapy has also been found to decrease blood pressure and to put children. at ease in the presence of a counselor.[4] Moreover, Yount, Olmert, and Lee indicate that oxytocin can help to moderate symptoms of PTSD, especially the hyperarousal symptoms and fear responses.[5] According to Chandler, the presence of oxytocin in our body can effect states of pleasure, relaxation, and calmness.[6] Oxytocin is known to be present during breastfeeding and sexual intercourse and is, therefore, believed to stimulate social attachment. Chandler also reports that oxytocin has been shown to be released after a stressful experience to help recover from the experience.

I and others believe that the psychological benefits of being and interacting with a furry facilitator include but may not be limited to clients' improved mood, self-esteem, confidence, and attachment to people. Other benefits relate to reductions in states of anxiety, agitation, and sadness.[7]

Moreover, I have seen and many authors have indicated that, elements of AAP that benefit clients can include providing entertainment, uplifting mood, helping clients to feel comforted, to identify an emotion, to soothe, to increase self-confidence, to focus attention, to be accepted in a non-judgmental manner, to increase self-

---

[4] Fine (2010); Rovner (2012); Shubert (2012b); Yount, Olmert, and Lee (2012).

[5] Yount, Olmert, and Lee (2012).

[6] Chandler (2012).

[7] Blum Barish (2002); Chandler (2005, 2012); Jalongo (2005); King (2007); Matuszek (2010); Minatrea and Wesley (2008); Parish-Plass (2008); Pichot (2012); Sacks (2008); Zamir (2006).

esteem, to master an object or an activity, and to improve reading skills.[8]

Again, I have seen in my own practice and agree with King, Jalongo, and Schultz, Remick-Barlow, and Robbins that AAP helps clients relax, increase their level of comfort, build trust, establish rapport and communication, learn new skills, normalize the therapeutic environment, reduce blood pressure and heart rate, and it can enhance the motivation of the client's participation in therapy.[9]

I also agree with the Delta Society's claims that animal-assisted therapy can help people to establish empathy, develop an outward focus, increase nurturing skills, establish rapport, feel accepted, be entertained, further socialization, increase mental stimulation, and that this therapy can provide physical touch as well as help to decrease heart rate and blood pressure.[10] I have seen many an anxious or distressed client unconsciously or without awareness reach across my couch to the furry facilitator lying close by for comfort and support during emotional processing.

Like Berry and others, I have also seen that AAP can impact a child's peer-to-peer relationships and

---

[8] Chandler (2005, 2012); Eggiman (2006); Fine (2010); Fike, Najera, and Dougherty (2012); Friesen (2010); Geist (2011); Golin and Walsh (1994); Gregg (2012); Hanselman (2001); Jalongo (2005); Jalongo, Astorino, and Bomboy (2004); King (2007); Lange et al. (2006); Minatrea and Wesley (2008); Peters (2001); Pichot (2012); Prothmann, Bienert, and Ettrich (2006); Rubenstein (2012); Schultz, Remick-Barlow, and Robbins (2007); Souter and Miller (2007).

[9] King (2007); Jalongo (2005); Schultz, Remick-Barlow, and Robbins (2007).

[10] The Delta Society (2000).

interactions with adults and that the therapy dog can act as an "emotional bridge" in therapy. [11]

Figure 5.1 Hobbes & Loki

Potential Benefits for the Client's Family

I firmly believe that benefits can also accrue to the client's family. These can be incidental or direct benefits, such as when a child is able to manage life better, which results in less stress for all family members. This result can mean that the family might be more likely to go out with the child because they might no longer feel embarrassed because the

---

[11] Berry et al. (2012).

child behaves better in social situations. Similarly, when a child becomes more verbal and able to interact more with family members, it creates a more cohesive family life.[12] An additional family benefit is when AAP results in better peer-to-peer relationships and child-to-adult relationships, as this result then provides the parents some hope that their child can and will be happy now and hopefully later in life. Finally, the family might benefit when they feel more connected to their child; see the story of Mark in Chapter 11.

Potential Benefits for the Therapist

Those of us who work in fields involving human-animal interactions are aware of the benefits we reap from working alongside a loving animal. For me and other therapists, the benefits include increased job satisfaction by having a loving pet to work with, connecting more to clients, experiencing fewer cancellations, and clients being more motivated to reach their goals.[13] I agree with King that benefits for clinicians can also include reducing stress and burnout, providing a less expensive way of having a co-therapist, and finally, as professionals are ethically and legally discouraged from touching clients, the therapy dog

---

[12] Ibid.

[13] Butler (2004); Chandler (2005, 2012); Lind (2009); Peters (2011); Peterson (1999).

provides a safe avenue for giving and receiving touch in therapy.[14]

I and other human-animal professionals also believe that the therapy dog benefits the therapist by increasing the therapy's effectiveness and by allowing the therapist to be more approachable.[15] When stressed from therapy work, the therapist can relieve burnout by petting the therapy dog or taking it for a walk.

Potential Benefits for the Therapy Dog

I think that there are many ways my therapy dogs benefit from their work. When my dogs know I am going to work, they will often race each other to the door, as if to say, "take me, I want to work." I believe, as do others, that therapy dogs benefit by engaging as a co-therapist, which relieves boredom for the dogs, provides stimulation, engages them mentally and physically, allows them to spend more time with the owner, promotes health and well-being, and encourages the therapy dog to be more connected to people. [16]

---

[14] King (2007).

[15] Chandler (2005, 2012); Fine (2010); Fike, Najera, and Dougherty (2012).

[16] Butler (2004); Chandler (2005, 2012); Fine (2010).

Risks of Animal-Assisted Psychotherapy

Any endeavor in therapy involves associated risks, and this is the case with AAP as well. Nonetheless, many of the risks involved with AAP can be minimized or prevented by proper risk-management policies and procedures. These risk-management strategies are discussed in Chapter 6.

Potential Risks Related to the Therapy Process

Generally, the therapy dog is present during sessions to provide comfort to a client when discussing a difficult experience. As long as the dog remains calm and sits beside the client, comfort can be provided. Nonetheless, my therapy dog Hobbes will sometimes react to clients' emotions by standing up, standing on their lap, and licking their face. Although this might be comforting if clients do not object to having their face licked, it can also disrupt the therapeutic process. In such situations Hobbes has turned tears into laughter, which might be a good thing, but as many therapists well know, it is important for clients, especially those impacted by trauma, to experience their emotions in connection to their life events. When this process is interrupted by the loving kindness of the therapy dog, it might potentially hinder the therapy process.

Nonetheless, it can also become a good teaching point, as clients can learn that intense emotions can be distracted, tolerated, or ended when something pleasant is experienced.

Another potential risk to the therapy process is when the therapy dog refuses to engage with a client who is seeking connection to the dog. In some cases, clients have expressed feeling rejected and hurt when my co-therapist refuses to engage with them. Again, although this behavior can be somewhat detrimental to the clients' psyche, this situation can also be used to challenge any irrational thoughts or beliefs that clients might express about themselves after being rejected by the furry facilitator.

Potential Risks for the Human Client

Specific risks to clients include possible injury, illness, attachment to the therapy dog, and potential grief or loss at the termination of services or if the animal retires or dies.[17] As Blum Barish states, "Even the most gentle and trusting animal may bite when in pain." [18]

In my private practice I have seen, as Chandler also indicates, that a potential risk to clients is when they become attached to the therapy dog and then experience grief or loss either at the termination of client services or if the therapy animal retires or dies.[19] This occurred in my own

---

[17] Chandler (2005, 2012); Fine (2010); Parshall (2003); Pitts (2005).

[18] Blum Barish (2002, p. 17).

[19] Chandler (2005, 2012).

practice when I retired Meika in 2011. See Chapter 13 for an example of this potential risk.

An additional risk is the appropriateness of AAP for particular clients. For instance, if a client has strong allergies or excessive fears related to dogs, these conditions make participating in AAP less beneficial and potentially harmful if the allergies or fears have not been successfully treated.[20]

Finally, another risk to the client is the possibility of becoming sick through contact with a therapy dog who is sick. This process is called zoonosis and is discussed later in this chapter.

Potential Risks for the Human Client's Family

Potential risks related to the human client's family involve any medical issues that might occur from an illness or injury caused by or passed from the therapy dog to the human client. Additionally, if a client is injured by the therapy dog, this could potentially result in a fear and/or phobia, which would then result in the need for more psychotherapy to treat the fear and/or phobia, all of which can place stress on the client's family. This stress can be both emotional and financial.

---

[20] Matuszek (2010).

Potential Risks for the Therapist

Potential risks for the therapist include stress in maintaining the safety and welfare of both the client and the therapy dog. Clients need to be protected from any possible injury or the transmission of an illness from the therapy dog. This risk requires the therapist to be watchful of the therapy dog to detect signs of stress and to maintain the therapy dog's health by having regular vet checkups.

To provide safety and welfare related to the therapy dog, the therapist must appropriately screen clients for abuse of animals and the clients' appropriateness for AAP. In many cases this is an easy task, but it can sometimes be complicated by the client's truthfulness and/or mental health issues.

Friesen indicates that cultural factors also play a role in the appropriateness or risk of engaging in AAP. Specifically, the provider of AAP should understand that in certain Middle Eastern and Southeast Asian cultures, dogs might be perceived to be "unclean," and therefore, interaction between a therapy dog and particular client is not recommended.[21]

Another potential risk to the therapist relates to the stress of making sufficient time to give the therapy dog a break. To maintain the dog's welfare, it is important that the therapist allow the therapy dog to take a break between sessions, without the therapist feeling stressed about such breaks. When therapy dogs or therapists become overly

---

[21] Friesen (2010).

stressed, it can weaken their immune system and can lead to ill health or negative behaviors.

Both humans and dogs can contract a virus or illness of some kind. When therapy dogs or therapists experience an illness, it is possible that they might pass this illness to another person or animal. This process is known as zoonosis.[22] This risk requires that therapists maintain their own health and the furry facilitator's health to prevent the occurrence of zoonosis.

Another risk for therapists is the derision of their colleagues, who might not understand or value the modality of AAP. As AAP is currently a nontraditional modality of treatment, many professionals are not aware of its complexity and value.[23] When I opened my private practice in Springfield, Virginia, my colleagues were somewhat cautious and concerned about liabilities potentially involved with the provision of AAP. Through education and my colleagues' willingness to accept the therapy dog into our offices, however, I have been able to maintain my AAP practice and have gained some respect for what AAP brings to the therapy process.

Friesen indicates that a common concern of therapists who provide AAP is the safety of children.[24] She states that others have noted the common occurrence of dog bites for children. and suggests that appropriate education to help children learn empathy for a therapy dog's unique requirements can help to prevent dog bites. This risk suggests that it is incumbent on those practicing AAP to

---

[22] Chandler (2005, 2012); Delta Society (2000); Fine (2010); Lefkowitz et al. (2005).

[23] Chandler (2005, 2012).

[24] Friesen (2010).

help our clients learn to interact with the therapy dog in a quiet and gentle manner, not, at least initially, in a playful and antagonizing manner. Practitioners of AAP should also teach clients when and how it is appropriate to approach a dog, including watching for signs of anxiety or aggression, and therapists should help people know how to behave if they are afraid of dogs. With Hobbes, who gets excited when people enter the room, I explain that he is using his emotional brain and that it helps him to use his thinking brain if we can be calm and assertive with him. I encourage clients to ask Hobbes to sit and for his paw, as this will distract him from his excitement and help him to become calm.

Friesen further suggests that to allay the fears of caretakers of children who may be treated using AAP, the caretakers might be more tolerant of AAP when they are allowed to see for themselves how well-groomed and obedient the animal is and how closely the interaction would be monitored by the counselor.[25] She further suggests that, before beginning AAP, therapists should respectfully communicate to caretakers the professional training both of the therapy dog and the counselor as well as the procedures and types of interactions likely to occur in order to obtain informed consent. In my practice, I meet with the parents or caretakers of the children I work with, allow them to ask questions, and demonstrate how well behaved my therapy dogs are. Once the parents have seen firsthand how well behaved the dogs are and how we work together as a team, I often hear and see a sigh of relief.

---

[25] Ibid.

Additional potential risks include legal ramifications if permission is not obtained or in case of injury to a client or another person. Another possible legal and ethical risk for therapists providing AAP is the use of an untrained or uncertified therapy dog. If the therapy dog has not at least undergone obedience training, the therapist could potentially be sued if the therapy dog were to harm a client or any person who comes to the facility where the therapist practices. Although obedience training for the therapy dog does not prevent someone from suing the therapist, a court might take into account that the dog was sufficiently trained and perhaps more likely to have been antagonized by the person who was harmed. When stressed or perceiving a threat, a dog can forget obedience training, and if the dog's human companion is not present to manage the situation, the dog will likely revert to its basic survival strategies to protect itself. Agencies such as Pet Partners (formerly the Delta Society), Therapy Dogs International, and other agencies that certify dogs for this work offer appropriate guidelines for preventing the mistreatment or burnout of therapy dogs. These guidelines and methods for reducing mistreatment or stress for the therapy dogs are discussed further below.

One way to minimize the legal liability for accidental injury caused by the therapy dog, according to Lange et al., is for therapists to "... consult both their professional liability insurance carrier and their homeowners' insurance agent to ensure they have insurance coverage for AAT."[26] The Trust Risk Management group of the American Psychological Association currently provides my

---

[26] Lange et al. (2006).

professional liability insurance, but they do not provide liability insurance for the provision of AAP. Additionally, therefore, for my private practice I have purchased a general business liability policy that does provide coverage for liability related to the therapy dogs causing an injury. I do not recommend using a homeowner's insurance policy to cover this, as that might cause further legal liability issues because this type of policy blurs the distinction between business and personal property.

Figure 5.2 Zoey at 5 months

Potential Risks for the Therapy Dog

The risks associated with AAP for the therapy dog include possible mistreatment of the animal, becoming stressed, and possible burnout.[27] The human therapist is responsible for preventing and managing these potential risks.

Eggiman indicates that therapy dogs can burn out and become very ill, experience chronic stress if not provided with sufficient breaks, and might even be overwhelmed or physically harmed by the human patients. Eggiman further states that when therapists work with children. who have been known to abuse animals, the therapy dog should not be introduced until the child is able to understand and abide by rules concerning safe interaction with the therapy dog.[28]

Ritchie and Amaker found that after a 24-month deployment to Iraq, a therapy dog, SFC Boe, appeared to have been traumatized by her work in the combat zone.[29] This traumatization required six weeks of retraining before SFC Boe was able to return to her therapy duties. Krol indicates that combat therapy dogs are now required to be re-evaluated upon their return from combat and prior to returning to their duties, to assess for any negative behaviors demonstrated by the dogs. In some cases, the combat stress dogs are retrained to assist in physical therapy with military personnel.[30] Another risk for combat theatre therapy dogs is potential disease transmission to the dogs resulting from contact with feral animals in combat areas.[31] Some authors also found that a potential hazard was that humans often gave treats to the therapy dogs, which

---

[27] Chandler (2005, 2010, 2012); Fine (2010); Lefkowitz et al. (2005); Parshall (2003).

[28] Eggiman (2006).

[29] Ritchie and Amaker (2012).

[30] Krol (2012).

[31] Ritchie and Amaker (2012).

resulted in their gaining weight.[32] Mental health providers also need to manage this risk, as obesity in dogs can have serious medical complications. For more information about risk management, see Chapter 6.

Zoonosis

Zoonosis is the transmission of diseases from animals to humans or from humans to animals. The most commonly recognized zoonotic diseases include West Nile virus (mosquitoes), SARS (severe acute respiratory syndrome, in mammals and birds), rabies (in dogs, foxes, wolves, coyotes, and other animals) avian influenza (birds), swine influenza (pigs), and Creutzfeldt–Jakob disease (mad cow disease). According to Capuzzi, there are approximately 1400 human infectious agents, and about 61% of those agents are zoonotic.[33] She indicates that children., pregnant women, the elderly, and those with a compromised immune system are at a higher risk for contracting a zoonotic disease. Zoonotic diseases can be caused by viruses, parasites, bacteria, fleas, and some forms of protein.[34] The most common zoonotic diseases are roundworms, ringworms, hookworms, and tapeworms. The diseases caused by these

[32] Fike, Najera, and Dougherty (2012); Ritchie and Amaker (2012).
[33] Capuzzi (2004).
[34] Dodds (2008); Pets Are Wonderful Support (2009); Scully (2011); USA Today (2005).

worms are hard to detect as they often mimic common illnesses.[35]

Generally, it is fairly difficult to contract a zoonotic disease from a therapy dog or from pets.[36] Many of the diseases that can be transmitted from dogs to humans are bacterial in nature. The most common method for the transmission of a dog's illness to a human is via a person touching infected feces. Some authors suggest that sleeping with our beloved pets can result in humans contracting a zoonotic disease.[37] Chomel and Sun indicate that about 50% of dog owners sleep with their dog, and they suggest that transmission of a zoonotic disease occurs when an infected animal licks or kisses a human.[38] In some cases the transmission of a dog's disease occurs when a human is bitten by another animal, such as a sand fly or tick, after the insect has bitten the dog. Of course, rabies can be contracted when an infected dog bites a human.

Zoonotic Diseases

Zoonotic diseases that can transfer from dogs to humans include salmonellosis, campylobacteriosis, and ringworm. Salmonellosis and campylobacteriosis are transmitted via infected feces and usually result in the human experiencing abdominal cramping, nausea, and diarrhea. Ringworm can

---

[35] Pets Are Wonderful Support (2009); Warner (1984).
[36] Pets Are Wonderful Support (2009).
[37] Chomel and Sun (2011; Scully (2011).
[38] Chomel and Sun (2011).

be transmitted by touching a dog that is infected with round, crusty lesions.[39] The photo below shows a dog that has ringworm.

Figure 5.3 Ringworm

Another zoonotic disease that can be transmitted from dogs via mosquitoes is dirofilariasis. Dirofilariasis can be asymptomatic in humans and might only be detected when lesions in the lung or subcutaneous nodules are found. Subcutaneous nodules can develop over several weeks and might be tender, painful, and red.[40]

Dogs can transmit roundworms to humans. Roundworms, or Toxocara canis, can affect two different areas in humans, when the young roundworms or larvae migrate to the lungs, liver, and muscles or when the larvae

---

[39] Capuzzi (2004); Matuszek (2010); Pets Are Wonderful Support (2009).

[40] Đorđević, Tasić, Miladinović-Tasić, & Tasić, A. (2010).

go to the eye. Canine hookworms can also be transmitted to humans and result in the human's gastrointestinal tract becoming infected with the hookworms.[41] As with hookworms and dirofilariasis, a human with roundworms can be asymptomatic for years. Nonetheless, common symptoms of both hookworms and roundworms include headache, nausea, vomiting, abdominal pain, and, in rare cases, jaundice.[42]

Another zoonotic disease is the transfer of canine tapeworms to humans. Symptoms related to tapeworms found in humans include diarrhea, abdominal pain, vomiting, weight loss, fatigue, constipation, and discomfort.[43]

A fungal infection on the skin of the human can also indicate a zoonotic disease. This is likely due to a dermatophyte (fungus) identified as Trichophyton mentagrophytes. This fungus can be transmitted via a dog bite. The fungal infection might take several months to appear and can also be seen on the dog that transmitted the fungus.[44]

Leptospirosis (aka Weil's syndrome or Rat Catcher's Yellows) is a bacterial infection transmitted to humans when dogs' urine contaminates soil or water. If the contaminated soil or water comes into contact with human skin or is ingested, the bacteria then infects the human.

---

[41] Chomel and Sun (2011); Dodds (2008); Pets Are Wonderful Support (2009); USA Today (2005).

[42] Ibid.

[43] Salb et al. (2008).

[44] Glaser (1998).

Leptospirosis is one of the most commonly transmitted zoonotic diseases.[45]

According to Warner and Matuszek, on military bases, the most common animal mite that infested humans was Sarcoptes scabiei var. canis, and the ringworm fungi was the most common fungi infecting humans from dogs.[46] Also according to Warner, pets can carry the bacteria Streptococcus, and this can result in children developing recurring strep throat.[47]

A form of meningitis caused by the bacteria Pasteurella multocida has been known to infect humans from a dog's oropharyngeal secretions via sniffing or licking. Another bacteria, the Capnocytophaga canimorsus, can infect a human when an infected animal licks a wound. This can be especially true when the human's immune system is compromised by asplenia or by alcohol or steroid dependence.[48] A previously well-known disease, which is currently uncommon, is the plague. In 2010, a case of the plague found in Oregon, USA, was determined to be caused by a dog licking and sleeping with a human. Nonetheless, the other human in the house was found to be positive for the plague serum (antibodies). The dog was later determined to be positive for Yersinia pestis, a bacteria known to cause the plague.[49]

Capnocytophaga canimorsus is another bacterial canine disease that can be transmitted via bites, licks, or sleeping with an infected canine. This illness can be more

---

[45] USA Today (2005).

[46] Warner (1984); Matuszek (2010).

[47] Warner (1984).

[48] Chomel and Sun (2011); Scully (2011).

[49] Scully (2011).

severe for those with an immune-compromised system or a pre-existing condition such as asplenia or alcoholism. Symptoms typically appear within about a week and include fever, vomiting, diarrhea, general discomfort, abdominal pain, muscle pain, confusion, shortness of breath, headaches, and skin rashes.[50]

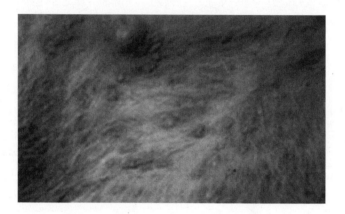

Figure 5.4 Staph Infection on a Dog

Humans can also transmit diseases to our pets and therapy animals. Such is the case of Methicillin-resistant Staphylococcus aureus (MRSA), commonly known as staph infection, which can cause pinkeye. It has been found that humans who were previously hospitalized for medical reasons, who have attended an outpatient clinic, or work in a health care setting are the most likely to infect an animal with MRSA.[51] The picture above shows a dog infected with a staph infection.

Another transmittable infection from humans to dogs and other animals is Giardia. The infection is

---

[50] Chomel and Sun (2011).

[51] Chomel and Sun (2011); Dodds (2008).

transmitted when an infected human defecates in water, which can contaminate water supplies or can be ingested by the animal.[52] The next chapter discusses the prevention of zoonotic diseases and other risk-management strategies.

---

[52] Dodds (2008); Pets Are Wonderful Support (2009).

Chapter 6

Animal-Assisted Psychotherapy: Risk Management

Meika was getting older, and her arthritis was getting more noticeable every day. In the mornings, when I got ready for work, her usual habit was to wait at the door, along with Loki, to see whom I would take to work with me that day. I noticed that, more often than not, I would have to call Meika to come so that we could leave for work. I knew in my heart, even though it saddened me, that she needed to stop working. I also knew, objectively, that because of her pain, she might growl one day when a child. played with her roughly. So, with much sadness I started the process of retiring Meika as a therapy dog. This meant, of course, telling my clients that this was going to happen and why. They would need to say good-bye to her, too.

The vignette above illustrates four areas concerning the risks and risk management of animal-assisted psychotherapy (AAP). The first is the risk for Meika. This risk pertains to her well-being and health. As she got older, she felt her age, as is usual for dogs. When she was reluctant to work because of age and/or pain, forcing her to work would stress her and was therefore more likely to lead to an unwanted behavior. Being objective about what I was seeing in Meika allowed me to understand what was best for her, for my clients, and for my practice, and such objectivity is an appropriate risk-management strategy. The potential risks to my clients and practice are the second and third risks and risk-management strategies illustrated in the vignette. Knowing that Meika was in pain made me more watchful of her, especially around children. This vigilance, of course, raised my stress level a little, which is the fourth risk to my efficacy. So, in deciding to retire Meika, I manage the risk of potential harm to her, to my clients, to my business, and to my own level of stress.

Risk Management for Clients

Risk management related to clients involves preventing or minimizing the possibility of injury. To prevent or minimize the possibility of injury, it is important to know the therapy dog well so that you read and understand the dog's signs of stress. When dogs are stressed, they can act unpredictably, which means they can bite. Another way to minimize this possible risk is to never leave the therapy dog alone with a client. When I work with children or adolescents and need to speak to a parent at the end of a session, I will ask the child or adolescent to bring the parent from the waiting room to my office. In this way, there is less likelihood that the child or adolescent will be harmed.

Another risk related to the client's well-being concerns the possibility of the client contracting an illness from the therapy dog. To minimize this risk, the therapy dog's vaccinations need to be up to date so that zoonosis is less likely to occur.

Another risk is when a client attaches to the therapy dog, which can potentially result in grief or loss at the termination of services or if the animal becomes sick, retires, or dies. Although this risk cannot be prevented, it can be ameliorated by addressing it with the client as it occurs or prior to its occurrence, if circumstances allow. When Meika retired in 2011, I began the process of telling clients of her imminent departure several months before she stopped assisting us. This was partly because I was also introducing Hobbes into our work. The advance notice allowed my clients ample opportunity to explore their reactions to her departure. Sometimes, when one of my therapy dogs becomes sick and I bring the other dog to work, clients might inquire about what happened, if they remember which dog they usually see in a particular week. Again, therapists can appropriately help clients to process and explore their concerns and thoughts regarding attachment to the therapy dog.

An additional risk related to clients is the appropriateness of AAP for particular clients. This risk can easily be managed by screening prior to working with or accepting a person as a client.

Risk Management for the Client's Family

The potential risks related to clients' families are similar to those of clients themselves, except that any injury or illness would happen to their loved family member who is being treated with AAP, which might cause emotional and financial distress to the family. The financial burden to the family involves caring for the client who has been harmed, which could necessitate medical and/or psychological care. Again, therapists who know their therapy dog's behaviors and medical conditions and who remain objective to the dog's conditions can easily manage these potential risks. If therapists keep these matters in mind, they can ameliorate any potential harm to both clients and their families.

Risk Management for the Mental Health Professional

First and foremost for all mental health professionals is the management of risk related to professional guidelines and ethics. All mental health professions require that practitioners be trained in the area or modality in which they practice. This agreement is also important with regard to AAP, as it is a relatively new modality for the treatment of mental health issues. Thus, those seeking to work in the modality of AAP will benefit by gaining knowledge and understanding of this modality. Reading books such as this one will help in that endeavor. Furthermore, obtaining additional training, such as that offered by Pet Partners, to understand the application of AAA/AAT is prudent.[1]

Chandler suggests that mental health professionals can mitigate several types of risks involved with AAP.[2] She states that these areas include but may not be limited to the appropriate socialization and training for the therapy dog and training for the mental health professional in animal-assisted interventions. Other risk-management factors that mental health professionals must consider include assessing the appropriateness of AAP for a particular client, possessing a basic understanding of zoonosis, (see Chapter 5 of this book), injury prevention, how to respond for both client and therapy dog when an injury occurs, being competent in establishing therapeutic goals and the ways in which AAP can facilitate those goals, and finally, continuously assessing whether therapeutic progress is being achieved, and adapting accordingly.

Another aspect of risk management includes obtaining appropriate informed consent for the client's participation in AAP. Most informed consent documents provide information regarding the professional's credentials, the type of services being provided, fees and cancellation policies, how to contact the counselor between

---

[1] Chandler (2012).
[2] Ibid.

sessions, the potential benefits and risks of therapy, information regarding AAP, any appropriate waivers, limits of confidentiality and duty to warn, and finally, signature and date lines for the client and therapist to acknowledge the informed consent. Chandler also indicates that informed consents may contain information regarding the therapist, how appointments are made and changed, the length of sessions (such as 45 minutes), the number of sessions being provided, the professional relationship between client and therapist, address and phone numbers for clients, and how health records will be disposed of in case of the therapist's death or after the client terminates therapy.[3]

Figure 6.1 Meika

---

[3] Ibid.

According to Chandler, an informed consent regarding AAP should also identify the type of animal involved, the training and any certifications the therapy animal has acquired, the relationship of the animal to the therapist, and the types of activities the therapy animal will engage in with the client, if the client chooses. Chandler further states that the informed consent paperwork should indicate that clients have the right to ask that the therapy animal not be present in their sessions.[4] This would, however, require that the therapist be able to transfer the therapy animal from the room to a safe place during this time. In my private practice, this is not something I can provide. Hence, when I screen to accept clients, I ensure that they are comfortable having a therapy dog in the room when we are working together. If clients decline this request, then I typically refer them to someone else.

Mental health professionals need to screen potential clients for their suitability for AAP. This screening is important because the person might have an extreme fear of the therapy animal, a severe allergy to the animal's fur, hair, or dander, might have been violent or abusive towards animals in the past, or might be in some way uncomfortable having a therapy animal in sessions. Screening for these issues is important both for the client, for the therapy animal, and for the therapist. Finally, some clients might not be appropriate for AAP due to a diminished capacity to understand the potential consequences of their actions. For example, if a child with autism is not able to restrain certain aggressive behaviors such as hitting or grabbing, s/he might not be appropriate for AAP as s/he might hurt or injure the

---

[4] Ibid.

therapy animal and in turn, the therapy animal might react in a way that injures or hurts the child.[5] Other clients that might not be suited to AAP include those individuals with impulse control difficulties, severe allergies to animals, and those with phobias of animals, specifically dogs.[6]

As Chandler suggests, mental health professionals must serve as advocates for their therapy animals. Specifically, she states that it is important that mental health professionals establish and maintain a healthy relationship with their therapy animal, continually monitor the therapy animal's ability to work in the capacity of a therapy animal, and provide a safe and comfortable environment for the animal to engage in AAP. Moreover, she states that when the therapy animal is not engaging in AAP, therapists should provide a comfortable, safe, and secure place for the animal, have a good understanding of the animal's behavior and an ability to interpret the animal's vocal and other behaviors, and finally, therapists should continually monitor the level of the therapy animal's stress and fatigue.[7]

In one article from the University of British Columbia, Okanagan, a teacher at the university who teaches about AAP, Binfet, noted that he does not advocate that everyone bring their dog to work, and he indicated that his therapy dog obtained advanced behavior certification and university approval before he brought him to work with the students.[8] Both these points are appropriate risk-management strategies.

---

[5] Ibid.

[6] Chandler (2005); Fine (2010); Wilkes (2009).

[7] Chandler (2012).

[8] University of British Columbia, Okanagan (2012).

Another important risk-management strategy is to minimize risk of injury to both the client and the therapy dog. This strategy can be achieved, at least in part, by keeping the therapy dog on a leash and by not leaving the client alone with the therapy dog. If however, the client is accidentally injured by the therapy dog or in some other way, it is important to secure the therapy dog, such as by putting it in its crate or in a place where the dog will lie down and stay so that you can focus on assisting the client to get medical attention.[9]

Mental health professionals should consider a well-developed plan in case of an accident or injury to the client or the therapy animal. The Pet Partners program, formerly the Delta Society, has developed a formal written plan in the event of an accident or injury to a patient or therapy animal. Chandler also stipulates that a well-developed written strategy for managing accidents and injuries is a prudent risk-management strategy.[10] Both Pet Partners and Chandler suggest that this plan include safely securing the animal, such as putting it in a crate or having it lie in a safe place, assessing the injury to the client or animal, providing assistance to the injured party, notifying any staff if appropriate, calling for medical assistance if necessary, and documenting the event. If the mental health professional is sponsored by any organization, such as the Pet Partners program, s/he should inform the organization of the incident.[11] Having a small first aid kit might also be helpful for this kind of situation.

---

[9] Chandler (2005; 2012); Fine (2010); Wilkes (2009).

[10] Chandler (2012).

[11] Chandler (2012); Delta Society (2000).

Another risk-management strategy is to carry professional liability and general liability insurance. Contact your professional liability insurance provider to determine whether they offer coverage for the practice of AAP. Initial or additional liability coverage can also be obtained through a general business liability insurance policy.

Risk Management Related to the Therapy Dog

Preventions for Zoonotic Diseases

As discussed in Chapter 5, zoonosis is a potential risk of AAP. The literature on AAP suggests that the process of zoonosis can be minimized by taking certain precautions, such as careful selection of the animal chosen to work as a therapy animal, ensuring that vaccinations and medications are up to date, especially those vaccines or medications that protect against ticks and fleas, providing regular health checks, ensuring that informed consent is in place, and washing hands after contact with a therapy dog.[12] Other precautions for preventing zoonosis include wearing shoes in areas where animals defecate and preventing young

---

[12] Cats, Dogs, and Other Medicine (2009); Chandler (2005, 2012); Fine (2010); Lefkowitz et al. (2005); Minatrea and Wesley (2008).

children from eating dirt, especially in areas where animals have likely defecated.[13]

Agencies such as Pet Partners, Therapy Dogs International, and Therapy Dogs, Inc. require a certification process for therapy dogs that makes it relatively difficult for a human to contract a zoonotic disease. This process requires that therapy dogs undergo yearly veterinary health exams to be inspected for roundworms, hookworms, ringworms, etc. and to maintain vaccinations and medications to prevent most known canine diseases, which include rabies, Lyme disease, canine distemper, adenovirus type 2 (a type of canine hepatitis), parainfluenza (kennel cough), parvovirus, heart worms, hookworms, roundworms, fleas, and ticks.

Recognizing the Animal Co-Therapist's Stress Level

It is very important to understand when a therapy dog is stressed. When dogs are stressed, they might act in unpredictable ways and might be difficult to control. So, it is important to understand the common signs of stress in your dog.

Signs of stress in dogs include but may not be limited to shaking, salivating, excessive blinking, restlessness, barking, whining, excessive grooming, refusing to accept treats, loss of appetite, turning away or avoiding

---

[13] Cats, Dogs, and Other Medicine (2009); Center for Disease Control (2010a, 2010b, 2010c); Dodds (2008); Sabry and Lofty (2009).

eye contact, licking lips, panting, yawning, shyness, dilated pupils, whining, pacing, lack of desire to socialize, hiding behind the therapist, or reluctance to get in or out of a vehicle.[14]

As occurs with humans, when a dog is stressed, the body can be flooded with hormones, such as adrenalin and cortisol. This reaction prepares the dog for a flight, fight, or freeze response.[15] It is important that therapists know and be aware of their therapy dog's signs of stress in order to ameliorate them as quickly and as effectively as possible.

Figure 6.2 A Relaxed and Tense Hobbes

In the pictures above, on the left, Hobbes is relaxed and calm. We can see this because his mouth is relaxed and open, his eyes appear relaxed, and his ears are attentive but

---

[14] Burch (1996); Chandler (2005, 2012); Delta Society (2000); Fine (2010); Lind (2009); McConnell (2002); Tellington-Jones (2012); Volhard and Volhard (2005).
[15] Tellington-Jones (2012).

not upright in an alert position. In the above picture on the right is another photo of Hobbes with his mouth closed, eyes tense and focused, ears alert, and notice the tension in his position, as if he were ready to jump up at any sound or movement.

Chandler indicates that it is important to know your therapy animal's signs of stress and how s/he communicates lack of interest or unwillingness to engage in therapy work. If we can remain objective about what we see in our therapy animals, these observations can help us to manage risks better.[16] With Meika, I had noticed toward the end of her therapy work, before she retired in 2011, that she was not as enthusiastic to go to work. Previously, when I would tell her, "Let's go work," she would rush to the door and pant excitedly to go, but later she would take her time going to the door and did not appear excited, only appeasing. If I had not heeded these and other signs that her arthritis was worsening, I could have created a risky situation.

Learning about how animals communicate and the meaning of their communication is a risk -management behavior. Books that can help you understand more about dogs' communications and behaviors include *The Other End of the Leash: Why We Do What We Do Around Dogs* by Patricia McConnell, Ph.D., and *Dog Training for Dummies* (2nd Ed) by Jack Volhard and Wendy Volhard.

---

[16] Chandler (2005, 2012).

Ameliorating the Animal Co-Therapist's Stress

Ameliorating the therapy dog's stress level begins with prevention. Methods for preventing stress include ensuring that dogs have sufficient breaks between activities or sessions and that they eat healthy food and exercise regularly.[17] I typically take my dog out for two to three breaks during the day, in which we go for a five to 10-minute walk. This also gives me a break. Additionally, as I have two working therapy dogs, I alternate them so that one works one day, has the next day off, and then works a second day for the week. As I work only four days a week, this schedule means that both dogs work only two days a week and have a long weekend between work weeks. Chandler indicates that a break allows the dog the time to relax, to stretch its muscles, and to relieve itself if needed, so it is prudent to carry materials to properly dispose of any of the dog's waste products.[18]

Other actions that reduce or prevent stress include petting and talking to the therapy dog soothingly. Between sessions, before the day starts, or at the end of the day, you might offer your dog a massage, with techniques such as the "Tellington TTouch."[19] Tellington TTouch are techniques that help dogs feel less stressed and fearful and can enhance

---

[17] Delta Society (2000); Lefkowitz et al. (2005); McConnell (2002); Volhard and Volhard (2005).

[18] Chandler (2005).

[19] Chandler (2005, p. 61).

the animal's relaxation and awareness.[20] If the stress signs continue, however, it might be best to allow the therapy dog to lie in a safe corner of the room quietly or to be taken home.[21] The latter is especially important if the dog vomits or becomes ill while working.

Krol indicates that the use of a "motivational object," such as a toy that the therapy dog enjoys, can be used to help ameliorate mild stress.[22] The toy can distract therapy dogs from whatever is stressing them and help them regain their focus.

---

[20] Tellington-Jones (2012).

[21] Butler (2004); Chandler (2005, 2012); Fine (2010); Lind (2009); Wilkes (2009).

[22] Krol (2012).

Chapter
7

Ethics Related to the Modality of Animal-Assisted Psychotherapy

Since starting my private practice and becoming known as an animal-assisted therapist, I am often contacted by mental health professionals about this modality. People often tell me that they are bringing their pet dog to their office and allowing it to interact with their clients and staff members in their workplace.

When I ask these professionals what books they have read about animal-assisted activities or therapy, they often tell me they have read nothing or perhaps a couple of articles about how the animals help to relieve stress. When I ask if they have attended any workshops or had their dogs assessed either for Canine Good Citizen behavior or as a therapy dog, they tell me "no." When I ask them what training they have in dog behavior or what books they have read, they typically tell me that they participated in an obedience class when they first acquired the dog. When I ask if they have received any clinical supervision for having their dog assist in therapy, they look at me with a blank expression.

When I ask them about the particular orientation they currently use in their therapy practice, what books they have read, what training they have undertaken, or any supervision they have received concerning the practice of therapy using this orientation, they typically list a number of books, articles, trainings, workshops, different supervisors they have had to help them become proficient in their modality of treatment. So then when I ask why they have not obtained all of this training for the animal-assisted psychotherapy (AAP) they are practicing, they sometimes look stunned, as if they had never considered this.

This scenario is common in my experience and clearly demonstrates the need for mental health professionals to be reminded of their ethics code related to the issues of "competence" in the services they provide. I also urge professionals to be mindful of the ethics related to animal welfare; thus, understanding dogs' behaviors and what their dog is reacting to is important, not just for the dog but also for the therapy work.

Ethics play an important part in providing therapeutic services to clients. A competent and ethical mental health practitioner will be compliant with the following: 1) any ethical code or standard of practice established by a particular area of mental health, such as the American Psychological Association Ethics Principals and Code of Conduct for psychologists; 2) all local, state, and federal guidelines and/or laws that govern the provision of mental health services to clients; and 3) standards and guidelines that are sensitive to cultural, racial, ethnic, and other individual differences. Additionally, when practicing in the area of AAP, one needs to comply with ethical codes and standards regarding animal welfare for the appropriate provision of AAA, AAT, and AAP. Nonetheless, it is important to note that many professional standards, codes, statutes and/or laws do not specifically address ethics related to the provision of AAP.[1]

Although there are no official practice standards related to the modality of AAP, there are overarching ethical standards and guidelines for all mental health professionals to do no harm and to provide some benefits to those with whom we work professionally. Mental health professionals are required to have competency in the areas in which they practice. I strongly agree with Chandler, who states that to be competent and to provide effective treatment when working in the modality of AAP, there are several areas for which professionals need to have

---

[1] Chandler (2012).

education, training, or supervision.[2] She states that to be competent to practice AAP, one must know its history and development, be able to explain the benefits, functions, and roles of AAP, use the modality of AAP in a manner consistent with appropriate counseling practices, and comply with the legal, ethical, and professional standards or guidelines related to AAP. It is also important that the therapist work as a team with the therapy animal and advocate for the therapy animal.[3]

Figure 7.1 Loki and Meika

Generally, ethics that are pertinent to a mental health practitioner working in the modality of AAP require that the practitioner consider balancing the needs of the human clients against respect for and the needs of the therapeutic animal and of the therapist.[4] The following pages explore in more detail the ethics of the modality of AAP related to the therapist, client, and therapy dog.

---

[2] Ibid.

[3] Ibid.

[4] Chandler (2005, 2012); Delta Society (2012); Fine (2010).

Ethical Issues Related to the Role of the Therapist

According to numerous researchers, it is important that any mental health worker practicing AAP be trained and knowledgeable about AAA and AAT.[5] Moreover, Chandler, Fine, Lange et al., and Minatrea and Wesley suggest that people bringing their pet to their office and allowing their animal/pet to interact in their professional capacity should be trained to understand how to manage risk and should be knowledgeable about AAP to avoid ethical issues related to practicing outside of one's competence.[6] Knowing when and when not to use the modality of AAP is an issue of competency.[7] Indeed, a practitioner who does not understand the various ways that AAP can enhance and facilitate therapeutic processes and growth would not be able to fully utilize the modality of AAP.[8] This lack of knowledge could be considered an "incompetency," as lay people might assume that the professional knows what s/he is doing, and therefore, in fact, one might construe that this knowledge is a mandated ethic of "competence." The American Psychological Association's (APA) Ethical Principles and Code of Conduct, Standard 2: Competence

---

[5] Chandler (2005, 2012); Chandler et al. (2010); Delta Society (2008, 2010, 2012); Fine (2010); Lange et al. (2006); Minatrea and Wesley (2008).

[6] Chandler (2005, 2012); Chandler et al. (2010); Fine (2010); Lange et al. (2006); Minatrea and Wesley (2008).

[7] Chandler (2012).

[8] Ibid.

states that "(Psychologists planning to provide services, teach or conduct research involving populations, areas, techniques or technologies new to them undertake relevant education, training, supervised experience, consultation or study."[9]

Just as therapists learn different modalities of treatment, such as Dialectical Behavior Therapy, Emotional Focused Therapy, or Eye Movement Desensitization Reprocessing, I believe it is necessary for those who wish to utilize the modality of AAP or even merely to bring their dog to their office to obtain training and competence in the field of AAP. I know that when I began this endeavor in 2003, it was hard to find any formal training. I devoured Levinson's and Fine's books as well as numerous articles to begin to understand the modality of AAP. Fortunately, now there are more books, articles, and even some formal programs to help professionals learn and become competent in providing AAP. I have listed below some of the available programs that help to address the issue of competence in AAP:

- American Humane Society
- Carroll College, Montana
- Oakland University
- University of Denver
- University of North Texas
- Animal-Assisted Therapy Programs of Colorado
- Professional Therapy Dogs of Colorado

---

[9] American Psychological Association (2003, 2010).

- Humane Society University, Washington, D.C.
- University of New Hampshire

See the Appendix for the contact information of the above programs and other agencies that provide training related to AAA, AAT, and AAP.

Chandler indicates that at a minimum, the therapist and therapy dog should be certified by Pet Partners, Therapy Dogs International, or Therapy Dogs, Inc. She also suggests that it would be prudent to obtain additional training beyond the minimal certification level to enhance professional AAP skills. Chandler states that additional training can help to reduce and to manage risks in providing AAP.[10] In my case, after being certified with Meika as an AAT team by the Delta Society, I was supervised by Dr. Chandler for one year while providing AAP.

According to Chandler, some states, such as Connecticut, have enacted laws that pertain to working in the modality of AAP.[11] Other states have laws that require appropriate documentation regarding the vaccinations and health conditions of the therapy animal, define a therapy animal, provide for the protection of the therapy animal, and specify access to public areas and transportation for therapy animals. It is therefore important for mental health practitioners to understand what their particular state laws allow, before they begin to provide services in the modality of AAP.

The Delta Society's code of ethics concerning AAA and AAT recommend specific actions that I also believe

---

[10] Chandler (2005, 2012).
[11] Chandler (2012).

that all mental health professionals providing AAP should follow:

Code of Ethics for AAA and AAT:

1. Perform duties commensurate with your position and training.
2. Abide by the professional ethics of your respective professions and organizations.
3. Demonstrate a belief and attitude of reverence for all life.
4. At all times, treat all the animals, the people, and the environment with respect, dignity, and sensitivity, maintaining the quality of life and experience for all involved.
5. Be informed and educated on the aspects and issues related to AAA and AAT.
6. Demonstrate commitment, responsibility, and honesty in all phases of your activities.
7. Comply with local, state, and federal laws and Delta Society Policies governing.[12]

The Delta Society also states that a person providing AAA or AAT is expected to behave in a professional manner and that unprofessional conduct, such as breach of confidentiality, abuse of a client or animal, theft, unauthorized use or possession of intoxicants, narcotics, or other drugs while volunteering as a Pet Partner, being unfit due to alcohol or drug abuse, and/or harassment of any type is not tolerated and will likely result

---

[12] The Delta Society (2012, p. 18).

in the termination of the person's participation in the Pet Partners program.[13]

Ethical Issues Related to the Client

One of the APA's ethical requirements stated in the Ethical Principles and Code of Conduct, standards, sections 3.10 and 10 is to obtain informed consent from clients for participation in therapy.[14] This requirement should also include obtaining informed consent for participation in AAP. In addition to the usual information contained in an informed consent, such as the therapist's credentials, service descriptions and charges, policies regarding appointments and cancellations, billing policies, termination policies, payment policies, and limits to confidentiality, a small paragraph regarding participation in AAP should also be included. My informed consent contains the following brief paragraph:

ANIMAL-ASSISTED THERAPY

Therapy focuses on developing ways to address your particular concerns about your life. Sometimes animals can aid therapy by helping us feel safe, loved, and accepted.

---

[13] The Delta Society (2012).
[14] American Psychological Association (2003, 2010).

Sometimes animals sense things that may be out of our awareness, and they react by attempting to connect with us, perhaps by putting their head on your lap or gently nudging you with their nose. This can be an animal's way of saying they know, understand, and want to help you. Animals can also help with developing social skills or self-care skills. Occasionally, when an animal does something, such as act scared, a person may identify with that feeling, and that becomes an opportunity to discuss what is happening for the client.

Of course, another ethical, risk-management, and legal issue related to clients is how to ameliorate the possibility of physical and psychological harm. Part of ameliorating potential physical harm to clients is to ensure that the therapy dog is healthy and vaccinated against most of the possible causes of zoonotic diseases, such as rabies, hookworm, roundworm, ringworm, Lyme disease, distemper, and parvo (see Chapters 5 and 6 for more information on zoonotic diseases and prevention). Mental health professionals can ameliorate potential physical harm to clients by ensuring that they have a well-trained and obedient therapy dog and by being aware of the dog's physical health. When even well-trained dogs are ill or stressed, they can behave out of character. See the risk-management strategies in Chapter 6 for more information. To ameliorate potential psychological harm to clients when utilizing AAP, again, it is prudent to have a well-trained and obedient therapy dog because in my opinion, it is likely that psychological harm to clients could occur only if they were physically harmed by the therapy dog. I cannot foresee any other way that psychological harm could befall clients when utilizing AAP.

Ethical Issues Related to the Therapy Dog

One of the first ethical issues to consider related to a therapy dog is health maintenance. Many programs and agencies, such as Pet Partners (formerly the Delta Society), Therapy Dogs, Inc., Therapy Dogs International, and many others stipulate that the minimum criteria for a dog to be assessed as a therapy dog is that its health be maintained through a proper diet, exercise, and regular health checkups. These programs and agencies also require that, at a minimum, the dogs be appropriately vaccinated and assessed by a veterinarian on an annual basis.[15] According to Chandler, there are state laws that pertain to this requirement.[16] These programs further require that a potential therapy dog be appropriately trained in behavior. At a minimum level, this will require that the dog be tested according to such guidelines as the American Kennel Club's Good Canine Citizen Certification. These agencies further require that a potential therapy dog be assessed for additional requirements related to the position of a therapy

---

[15] Burch (1996); Butler (2004); Chandler (2005, 2012); Fine (2010).
[16] Chandler (2012).

dog.[17] Although none of these items are required by any mental health professional organizations, such as the American Psychological Association or the Association of Social Work Boards, these requirements are prudent ethical and risk-management objectives for people choosing to work with animals in their profession.

Zamir indicates that the following ethics are appropriate for anyone engaging in AAA, AAT, or AAP activities:

1. The human companion/therapist's priority is the animal's welfare;
2. No force should be used to make the therapy animal leave its home or perform any task;
3. The therapy animals must be allowed to rest; and
4. The therapy animals must be protected from individuals carrying diseases that can spread to them.[18]

Preziosi agrees with Zamir's four ethical points and adds nine more ethical considerations related to the therapy animal. These ethical considerations include the following:

1. The therapy animal should never be forced to leave its home to perform AAP work;
2. Practitioners should know their therapy animal well enough to recognize when it is not comfortable and should not place the therapy

---

[17] Chandler (2005, 2012); Fine (2010).
[18] Zamir (2006).

animal in situations where it might be uncomfortable;

3. Practitioners should gradually acclimatize the therapy animal to whatever travel is necessary for it to perform AAP;

4. All activities engaged in by the therapy animal are safe and enjoyable for the therapy animal;

5. The therapy animal should always remain with or in sight of the practitioner during professional activities;

6. Practitioners should ensure a safe professional working environment for the therapy animal;

7. Practitioners should ensure that the therapy animal does not receive any food or is offered any food without the express permission and supervision of the practitioner;

8. Practitioners should ensure the health and vaccination of the therapy animal; and

9. Practitioners should demonstrate respect for the therapy animal and should in no way "use" the therapy animal.[19]

Zamir and Fine indicate that exposing therapy dogs to strangers who pet them can create stress for the dogs.[20] Fine further states that therapy dogs should be allowed to seek this intimate touch rather than it being forced on them.[21] Fine and Zamir also posit that, although working as a therapy dog can enhance the dog's life, it is also important

---

[19] Preziosi (1997).

[20] Fine (2010); Zamir (2006).

[21] Fine (2010).

for the therapist to know when the dog is ready to retire, does not want to work, or should not work due to medical issues.[22] This situation occurred with Meika in 2011, when I noticed that her arthritis was worsening, and she seemed less motivated to work. I then began to introduce Hobbes to therapy work and limited Meika's work time. Eventually, by the end of 2011, Meika retired from her therapy dog work.

According to Chandler, some animal welfare organizations are concerned about the participation of animals in activities such as AAP as they consider the ethics of abusing or exploiting the animals.[23] She reports on studies that looked at these issues; one found that for some therapy animals in elder care facilities, the work resulted in their being fed too much and exercised too little, which causes significant medical problems for the animals. Another study determined that in some residential facilities, the therapy animals were not allowed sufficient rest, and some animals were physically abused while kenneled. Finally, these studies found that, for therapy animals that visited facilities, these visits stressed the animals, which again indicates that appropriate avenues for stress relief are important for the therapy animals.[24]

According to Parish-Plass, when therapists provide AAP to a child, it is important that they ensure safety for all concerned, promote developmentally appropriate interactions between the child and therapy dog so that the child can emotionally handle the interaction, and when

---

[22] Fine (2010); Zamir (2006).
[23] Chandler (2005).
[24] Ibid.

aggressive or violent themes arise in the child's projective play, therapists. should ensure that no emotional or physical harm occurs to the therapy dog.[25]

Many authors have articulated other important ethical considerations for working in the modality of AAP. These areas include but may not be limited to protecting the therapy dog from abuse, stress, and discomfort, failing to be sensitive to the needs of the therapy dog, placing the human's needs over those of the animals, companions/therapists lacking the capacity to sublimate their own ego while working in the modality of AAP, proper health care for the therapy dog, providing a quiet place for the therapy dog, and "using" the therapy dog instead of treating the therapy dog as a partner.[26] An example of the need to be sensitive to the therapy dog's needs is when the dog reacts to a client's emotions, such as when my therapy dog Loki tries to hide when a client becomes angry. If I were to prevent him from taking refuge, force him to be with the client, or fail to ask the client to moderate anger for the sake of Loki, I would likely be acting unethically.

Ethical considerations also include providing a break from work activities not only between work days but also during each working day, such as allowing the therapy dog to choose not to interact and to go off into a quiet corner of the room to lie down and rest.[27]

---

[25] Parish-Plass (2008).

[26] Burch (1996); Chandler (2005, 2012); Delta Society (2008); Fine (2010); Friesen (2010); King (2007); Lind (2009); Pichot (2012); Wilkes (2009).

[27] Burch (1996); Chandler (2005, 2012); Fine (2010); Friesen (2010); King (2007); Wilkes (2009).

Therapists must also really know and understand their therapy dog and its behavior. This item is important because when therapists know the therapy dog well, they are then able to reliably predict and control how the therapy dog will react in certain situations.[28] For example, my therapy dog Loki does not like to have his paws grabbed. If his paws are grabbed, he will emit a low growl and pull the paw away. If this behavior were to happen in a therapeutic context, his growl might be seen as threatening. Yet, understanding and knowing how Loki will react, I can inform clients that they must ask to touch Loki's paws and not simply grab them, as he might display discomfort. This situation will be discussed later in the book in terms of the therapeutic role modeling of appropriate touch. Nonetheless, having trained all of my therapy dogs to be able to accept some mild rough touch, I can be confident that if a client pets them roughly, the dogs will not react negatively to this touch.

---

[28] Fine (2010).

Chapter
8

Choosing and Preparing a Puppy or Dog to be a Therapy Dog

Choosing a puppy or dog as a companion is an important choice. This choice is even more important when selecting a puppy or dog to be a potential therapy dog. Typically, people choose a dog based on their emotional reaction to the dog, such as feeling sorry for it or loving its cuteness. As therapists choosing a puppy or dog, we cannot base our decision on the puppy or dog's cuteness or sadness. We need to be completely objective about choosing the animal. Moreover, in some cases, due to the stigmatization of a particular breed of dog, such as pit bulls, we might need to consider the appropriateness of the dog's breed and our clients' reactions to it. Unfortunately, the bad press some breeds have been subjected to will likely cause clients, particularly children, to be potentially more scared of such a dog, and that makes the therapy animal's job harder to do, which can create a barrier to the therapy process.

Figure 8.1 Loki

Before selecting a dog for therapy work, it is prudent to learn and understand the fundamentals of dog behaviors so as to know how to recognize and assess your potential therapy dog's behaviors and temperament.[1] It is also important to know as much as you can about the dog's history, including both medical and life experiences, if possible.[2] Fine states that it is important that a therapy dog be emotionally mature so that s/he has had time to develop emotional control.[3] A young, immature dog will likely have

---

[1] Chandler (2012); Fine (2010); McConnell (2002); Miller (2010); Sacks (2008); Volhard and Volhard (2005); Yeager and Irwin (2012).

[2] Chandler (2005, 2012); Fine (2010); McConnell (2002); Volhard and Volhard (2005).

[3] Fine (2010).

difficulty controlling impulses. Moreover, understanding how dogs learn is helpful for training the dog.[4] Finally, Chandler indicates that having in-depth knowledge of animal-assisted psychotherapy (AAP) can help with selecting an appropriate animal for therapy work.[5]

Recognizing the Animal Co-Therapist's Attributes

So what makes a good therapy dog? First and foremost is the dog's temperament. The dog's temperament should be one that is attuned to people, calm, friendly, and a little curious. It is important that the dog be interested in people; otherwise, the dog will unlikely interact well in a therapeutic setting. The therapy dog needs to be calm. An anxious dog will not necessarily engage with clients, especially if the dog is fearful of people. The therapy dog needs to be friendly towards children., adolescents, adults, males, females, people of diverse ethnic origins or racial groups, people in wheelchairs, and people on crutches. In other words, the therapy dog should be friendly and engaging with all types of people. The dog's curiosity will help the animal to become engaged with clients and want to interact. It is also important to understand that dogs are able to detect human emotional states and, in some cases, even prior to an

---

[4] Alers and Simpson (2012); McConnell (2002); Yeager and Irwin (2012).

[5] Chandler (2012).

individual's awareness of his/her emotions. If the therapy dog has this natural ability and is encouraged to demonstrate it, this can be therapeutically beneficial.[6]

Tests and Assessments for a Potential Therapy Dog

Chandler describes a few quick tests that you can easily perform to assess whether a mature dog might be a good therapy dog.[7] She indicates that if you quickly move a hand towards the dog's face, stopping about a foot from the dog's nose, and the dog does not cower from you, or if you wave your hand in front of the dog's face, again about a foot away, and the dog does not move away, then s/he is likely a good candidate for being a therapy dog. To test the dog's sociability, Chandler recommends calling the dog to come while you are standing; if you need to crouch to get the dog to move towards you, then s/he is likely not a good candidate for a therapy dog.[8] She also suggests that a good test to see whether the dog can acclimate to loud noises is to clap your hands loudly once and observe the dog's reaction.

If you are looking to obtain a puppy to train to be a therapy dog, Chandler indicates five easy-to-perform tests

---

[6] Burch (1996); Chandler (2005, 2012); Fine (2010); Lind (2009); McConnell (2002); Reichert (1998); Volhard and Volhard (2005).

[7] Chandler (2005, 2012).

[8] Chandler (2005).

to assess the animal.[9] First, she states, watch the puppy's interactions with his/her littermates. If a puppy that is at least 7 weeks old seeks interaction, plays well with littermates, and is not overly aggressive, rough, fearful, or submissive, then the puppy appears to be a good candidate for a therapy dog. The other four tests should be conducted in a small, contained area away from littermates and other animals. Two of the tasks assess the puppy's sociability. First, clap your hands and call the puppy to you; as the puppy walks away, call him/her again. If the puppy returns to you again and again, this behavior demonstrates a puppy that enjoys interacting socially. The second test for social capacity is to hold and play with the puppy, and if the puppy seeks to cuddle with you, lick your face or another body part, and appears affectionate, then these qualities indicate that this puppy is likely to be a good therapy dog.

Figure 8.2 Hobbes & Zoey

---

[9] Ibid.

The last two tests relate to the puppy's dominance and reactions to unusual stimuli. A puppy that is willing to submit to human dominance is likely to make a good therapy dog. Chandler describes the test of dominance as gently placing the puppy on his or her back and rubbing the chest for a few moments.[10] If the puppy submits, then we have a good candidate for a therapy dog. The final exercise is to test the puppy's fearfulness. To do this, place a few pebbles or small coins into an empty soda can and tape the hole shut. The soda can is then gently tossed about two to three feet away from the puppy; be careful not to get too close or to hit the puppy with the can. A normal puppy's reaction is to be somewhat startled by the loud noise and then to be curious. If the puppy turns toward the noise and then walks over to the can, then we have a puppy that appears not to be fearful. This reaction or behavior is a good attribute for a potential therapy dog.

With regard to adopting a shelter or rescue dog for the purposes of AAP, Chandler states that, as you cannot know the history of this dog, whether it has been abused, or other factors that might impact its ability to be a therapeutic animal, you will need to assess for attributes that suggest that this animal has the potential to be a therapy dog.[11] Volhard and Volhard state that this evaluation should consist of assessing the shelter/rescue dog's ability to be restrained and dominated socially and to retrieve an object.[12] Specifically, they state that to assess for the dog's ability to be restrained, place the dog in the "down" position, gently

---

[10] Chandler (2005, 2012).

[11] Chandler (2012).

[12] Volhard and Volhard (2005).

roll the dog onto his/her back, and hold the dog there. If the dog struggles consistently, jumps up, or becomes aggressive, this indicates that the dog is not a good candidate to be a therapy dog.[13] However, if the dog squirms a little intermittently but remains on its back, then it is likely to be a good therapy dog. To test the social dominance of the dog, the authors indicate that, directly after the restraint test, you should sit close beside the dog, stroking it and placing your face close to the dog while talking softly; if the dog, immediately after being restrained, licks you and appears to accept your behaviors, s/he would likely be a good therapy dog. Finally, Volhard and Volhard suggest that testing whether the dog will bring you an object also indicates whether the dog can be trained. They suggest that throwing a small object approximately six feet away and encouraging the dog to bring it back to you is a good test to determine whether the dog can be trained.[14]

Other Matters to Consider for a Potential Therapy Dog

A dog with any of the above characteristics can make a good therapy dog, so the breed of the dog is not necessarily important. What is important to consider is the dog's size and the setting in which the dog will assist with therapy. For instance, in a private practice with a small office, it might

---

[13] Ibid.
[14] Ibid.

not be prudent to have a large, 100-pound dog. However, if your facility can accommodate a large dog in that there are large rooms or the interactions with the therapy dog will take place outside in a fenced area, a large dog might be well suited to that facility.[15]

Figure 8.3 Hobbes Sleeping at 14 weeks

As stated in previous chapters, however, it is also important to know the dog well and to understand his/her communications and signals. Our assessment of signals and behaviors must remain objective. If we fail to remain objective in viewing our therapy dog's behavior, we might miss some important signs of stress, and then the therapy dog might behave inappropriately.[16]

Last but not least, the dog needs to be socialized and trainable. This is important, as you will see later in the

---

[15] Burch (1996); Chandler (2005); Fine (2010); Lind (2009).

[16] Burch (1996); Butler (2004); Chandler (2005, 2012); Fine (2010); Lind (2009); McConnell (2002).

book.[17] According to Chandler, for puppies and dogs to become therapy dogs, they need to be properly socialized, desensitized to touch, have basic obedience skills, and if possible, know some tricks or have some special skills.[18]

Socializing, Desensitizing, and Training the Animal Co-Therapist

Socializing the Animal Co-Therapist

A therapy dog should be socialized in many different situations and settings. The therapy dog needs to be exposed to old and young people alike, different genders, different racial groups, and a variety of situations involving noise, rapid movement, or other distracting activities. Additionally, people come in all sizes and shapes and wear various clothing styles. People can also smell very differently. This is important because the dog's primary sense is the sense of smell. It is therefore a good idea to socialize your potential animal co-therapist with these different aspects of people.[19] Having the potential therapy dog become accustomed to people wearing hats, gloves,

---

[17] Burch (1996); Butler (2004); Chandler (2005, 2012); Fine (2010); Lind (2009); McConnell (2002); Wilkes (2009).

[18] Chandler (2005).

[19] Chandler (2005, 2012); Fine (2010).

using a purse, crutches, wheelchairs, and so forth, is helpful to prevent stress in the dog.

Moreover, it is likely that your animal co-therapist will come to your work situation in a car, so it is important to socialize the animal to being in a vehicle, behaving well, and not becoming stressed from the drive. Having the potential therapy dog, starting from a young age, become accustomed to getting in and out of a vehicle as well as traveling in the vehicle is thus a good socialization process.[20]

Furthermore, as in my case, having more than one pet requires that potential therapy dogs be socialized to spending time away from their "pack." For this situation, it is practical to have each of the potential therapy dogs spend time away from the home and the other animals they know. Socializing the dogs by taking them to your office for a few minutes a few times a week and having them get used to being in your location and meeting people is helpful.[21] The therapy dog should also be socialized with many other types of animals. This is particularly important when the agency providing AAT or AAP has many types of animals in the practice.

Another part of the socialization process involves acquainting your potential therapy dog with various activities, noises, situations, and places. Many pet stores, garden centers, hardware stores, and some restaurants allow dogs on their premises. Socializing your potential therapy dog in these places can relieve stress when s/he is working as a therapy dog. The sections below explain how to achieve this socialization.

---

[20] Chandler (2005, 2012).

[21] Chandler (2005, 2012).

Desensitizing the Animal Co-Therapist to Touch, Smells, Noises, and Sights

Desensitizing to Touch

Human Touching the Dog:

Because various types of people will likely pet or touch the animal co-therapist, possibly in many different situations, it is important to help the dog become accommodated to touch. This training should begin at an early age and continue throughout the dog's life. One way to accomplish this training is by petting the puppy/dog or by providing a daily massage.[22] As mentioned above, there is a technique referred to as the "Tellington TTouch" massage. According to Tellington-Jones, the Tellington TTouch touch involves circular, one-and-a-quarter circular motions of touch that can help reduce stress and fear in dogs as well as improve relaxation, alertness, intelligence, and the ability to be trained.[23] Chandler indicates that making small circles with the tips of your fingers on the surface of the dog's skin can facilitate desensitization to touch.[24] She also recommends that, while doing these circular motions, one should repeat a phrase in a quiet, calm voice to help relieve any tension or stress in the therapy dog. With my own dogs, I use a similar

---

[22] Ibid.

[23] Tellington-Jones (2012).

[24] Chandler (2005, 2012).

technique and use the word "calm," which is expressed in a low, long manner, so that it sounds like "caaaaaalmmm."

Additional training includes what I call "mauling" the dog. This consists of gently pulling on the dog's ears, legs, paws, and/or tail. When dogs are used to this kind of touch, they are less likely to react negatively should a person touch them in a rough manner.

Butler, Fine, and McConnell indicate that most dogs will misunderstand a person hugging them and might interpret this action as a threat and react negatively.[25] Therefore, it is important to consider and know a dog's behaviors in comparison with human behaviors, such as hugging. We can then work toward training the therapy dog to be able to accept a hug, if the dog's temperament allows. Fine and McConnell also indicate that appropriate training for dogs involves successive approximations of a behavior with positive reinforcement for any step toward the desired behavior.[26]

Dog Touching the Human

I also train the dogs to not mouth hands. A natural instinct for a young dog is to mouth objects, just as a human infant mouths objects. Training the dog to resist its natural urge to mouth objects is achieved by repeatedly placing a hand or object into the mouth of the dog. This action should be accompanied by a phrase, such as "drop it," until the dog learns to refrain from mouthing the hand or object or to turn his/her head away or push the hand away using the

---

[25] Butler (2004); Fine (2010); McConnell (2002).
[26] Fine (2010); McConnell (2002).

tongue. With this method, initially, dogs and especially puppies will mouth the hand or object; when this happens, the trainer should make a yelping sound. The dogs begin to learn that mouthing is not something they should do. Eventually, replace the yelping noise with a phrase spoken calmly, such as "drop it." These mauling and mouthing techniques are particularly useful when the therapy dog will be working with children. Often, children might intentionally or unintentionally pull on the dog's ears, legs, paws, and/or tail. The training thus desensitizes the therapy dog to these types of behaviors typical of children. The training to not mouth a hand is also important in case an accident occurs, such as if a person were to fall and the person's hand were placed in or near the dog's mouth. This skill is also important for dogs to learn so that when they are offered treats, they do not mouth the person's hand but rather gently take the treat with their lips and tongue, not with their teeth.

Desensitizing to Smells, Noises, and Sights

To desensitize a potential therapy dog to various smells, noises, and sights, it is necessary to socialize the animal with as many different places, people, and objects as you can. Take the dog-in-training to parks, shopping areas, and as many businesses or locations as possible. Walking dogs past a construction site can particularly help them become accustomed to unusual noises, sights, and smells. If you notice any stress in the potential therapy dog, then you should simply back away from the area until the dog becomes accustomed to these sights and sounds. Then, in subsequent days, encourage the dog to come closer and closer to this area, as comfort permits.[27] Ask people to work with you to help train the dog, for instance by asking them to get the dog to sit and to be petted or brushed, provided the dog is already used to these activities. Asking friends and family members to interact with the dog is also useful, for obvious reasons. Taking the dog to dog parks is a great way to socialize to different smells, noises, and sights. Walking dogs past ethnic restaurants also helps them get used to some unusual smells. Having them see and be around wheelchairs, walkers, and canes helps them become accustomed to seeing people using different ambulatory methods. Really, socializing the potential therapy dog to as many situations as you can is idea.

Training the Animal Co-Therapist

Obedience Training

It is very important to have therapy dogs undergo obedience training.[28] The basic commands of obedience training are to heel, come, sit, stay, lie, and the release from staying. In training the therapy dog to be obedient, these commands help to determine three important facets of the dog's behavior. First, obedience training helps therapists to understand and feel confident that they can rely on their

---

[27] Chandler (2005, 2012).

[28] Alers and Simpson (2012); Chandler (2005, 2012); Fine (2012); Fike, Najera, and Dougherty (2012); Foreman and Crosson (2012); Lange et al. (2006); Lind (2009); McConnell (2002); Sacks (2008); Volhard and Volhard (2005); Yeager and Irwin (2012).

dog's behavior in many situations. Second, when a therapy dog is fully obedience trained, the therapist can control the dog's behavior in most situations. Finally, obedience training helps the therapist to know how to predict the therapy dog's behavior in various situations. When the therapy dog's behavior is reliable, controllable, and predictable, we can reduce the risks of harm to the dog and to others.

Before you even begin to think about obedience training with your potential therapy dog, you must understand your dog's body language, stress signals, and calming signals.[29] This knowledge can be invaluable for obedience training. A dog that is stressed means that learning skills or being obedient is harder, so knowing your dog's stress signals can help you stop the training or manage the dog's behavior. Also, knowing if the dog is willing to engage by assessing the dog's body language will determine if learning can occur.

Volhard and Volhard indicate three main areas or drives in a dog that can determine how trainable the dog will be.[30] These are the prey, pack, and defense drives, with the defense drive further subdivided into fight and flight drives. Of the four drives, the most important for a therapy dog and for obedience training in general is a high pack drive. The pack drive is important because it indicates the dog's ability to live by rules and to be part of a group, including understanding the social hierarchy of who is the leader of the pack. The prey drive consists of behaviors associated with hunting, killing, and eating. Some prey

---

[29] Burch (1996); Chandler (2005, 2012); Fine (2010); McConnell (2002); Tellington-Jones (2012).
[30] Volhard and Volhard (2005).

behaviors such as jumping need to be discouraged, whereas other prey behaviors such as fetching should be encouraged in a therapy dog. Regarding the defense drive of fighting, this behavior must be assessed before considering whether the dog is suitable as a therapy dog. Particularly, the fight behaviors of not wanting to be petted or groomed, growling, and guarding food or toys are not appropriate behaviors for a potential therapy dog. Similarly, the flight behaviors demonstrated by lack of confidence, dislike of being touched by strangers, running away from new situations, or urinating when greeted by a stranger also make a dog unsuitable to be a therapy dog.

Accordingly, a dog with a high pack drive and low prey drive is an ideal candidate for a therapy dog, as this type is easily trainable. If the potential therapy dog has a high fight drive, you will need to be effective at establishing your leadership position. This is also true of a dog with a high prey drive. If your potential therapy dog has high prey and fight drives, it is likely that you will need professional assistance in training the dog to be obedient.[31] Nonetheless, it is also likely that a dog high in both prey and fight drives might not make a good therapy dog.

There are numerous methods for obedience training dogs, such as the clicker method (a form of operant conditioning), classical conditioning, positively reinforcing desired behaviors, operant conditioning, negative reinforcement for unwanted behaviors combined with positive reinforcement of desired behaviors, Cesar Milan's methods, and many other methods. Alternatively, you can work with a dog trainer who might have developed his/her

---

[31] Volhard and Volhard (2005).

own method of dog training. My experience in training my four dogs is that one size does not fit all. Loki, Hobbes, and Zoey were all very adept at learning from positive reinforcement – operant conditioning, with rare use of negative reinforcement. In contrast, Meika's style of training involved some positive reinforcement with food, but she is a relational kind of dog and did more to please than to receive a treat or food reward. Thus, she was often praised for her desired behaviors and scolded for her unwanted behaviors.

One of the first challenges in training is to have the potential therapy dog walk beside you on a loose leash and perform the heel command. One of the most common behavioral problems for dogs is pulling on their leash. This behavior is stressful not only for the owner but also for the dog. When dogs pull on their leash, they stress their backs, necks, shoulders, hips, and knees.[32] Correcting this problem requires that you have an appropriate collar and use a "check." The check consists of a crisp snap of the leash followed by an instant release in its tension. It is important that the dog find the check unpleasant; otherwise, this problem behavior will continue.[33]

The next basic obedience behaviors for the dog to learn are to sit, stay, lie, come, paw, and so forth. The dog can learn these behaviors through successive approximations for shaping the behavior. This technique is a basic Skinnerian behavioral modification method that most mental health professionals likely know. Another method for training the naturally occurring dog behaviors

---

[32] Tellington-Jones (2012).
[33] Volhard and Volhard (2005).

of sit, lie, and come is to say the word as the dog is naturally behaving in the desired manner. For instance, as you notice the dog is about to sit, you would then say the sit command and give any hand signal that you wish to connect to that behavior. The hand signal I chose for the sit command is to bring one or both hands to the chest so that the arms are bent at the elbows. I chose this hand signal as I have often seen young children performing this action as an animal that they fear somewhat approaches. So, if a child is fearful of the therapy dog and naturally makes this hand gesture, the therapy dog will react by sitting. Although children might not understand what has just happened, they are likely to feel less fearful when they notice that the dog is sitting and waiting for them to approach.

Tellington-Jones suggests that the best method of training is to keep exercises short, proceed one step at a time, use a variety of activities to teach a behavior, and use generous praise techniques such as touch, a happy voice, and treats.[34] Always watch the dog's body language, and if the dog is nervous or aggressive, do not stare into the dog's eyes because this behavior can be seen as a threat. Similar to Chandler, I train my therapy dogs to respond to non-verbal commands, such as hand signals.[35] This training can be invaluable when the room is noisy or your dog is far away. This is also important as dogs are naturally more visual, which is why they respond so well to non-verbal cues, such as hand signals and tone of voice.

Burch indicates that in addition to obedience training, a dog might need to be assessed in other ways.[36]

---

[34] Tellington-Jones (2012).
[35] Chandler (2005, 2012).
[36] Burch (1996).

She indicates that dogs need to be well socialized and trained not to jump on people. Therapy dogs also need to be responsive to commands such as "leave it" so that when they are attracted to something completely inappropriate for them to eat, smell, or urinate on, they will quickly move away and not perform that behavior. Finally, she indicates that therapy dogs should be able to tolerate other animals in their presence.

Alers and Simpson, in their article describing Dog Tags, which is a three-tier training program for soldiers to learn about and train dogs as therapy dogs, indicate how important it is for humans to understand the fundamentals of dog behaviors in order to better train the therapy dog.[37] The authors also report that the soldiers benefit from this program by increasing their self-esteem and confidence and by reengaging with their community. In the first tier of the program, the soldier first learns about philosophies of dog training and how to read dog body postures.[38] They also learn in the first tier how to train dogs in the basic obedience tasks of sit, stay, come, and heel as well as tricks such as paw, roll over, and having the dogs crawl on their belly. Finally, in the first tier, the soldiers learn how to positively motivate dogs for their training and later for their work. Alers and Simpson report that in the second tier, soldiers learn how to correct a dog's maladaptive behaviors, such as chewing, soiling, and jumping up.[39] These are important behaviors for dogs to have mastered before they can be certified as therapy dogs. In the last and third tier of the Dog Tags program, the soldiers, if they choose, can

---

[37] Alers and Simpson (2012).

[38] Ibid.

[39] Ibid.

learn more about developing techniques to help remedy complex behavioral problems in dogs.

Special Tricks or Skills for the Animal Co-Therapist to Learn

Although obedience training is very important and necessary for therapy dogs, additional training can include helping the dog learn tricks. Tricks such as paw/shake, roll over and roll back, leave it, stand, up, down, off, take it, fetch, high five, back (walk backwards), balancing a treat on the nose and waiting for the command to have the treat, drop it, wait, crawl, speak, giving a hug or kiss, and "stick 'em up" (a variation of the beg command) can all be used in therapeutic ways and as interventions. Chandler also recommends teaching tricks such as "say hello," "kennel," "place," "jump," and "find it" to therapy dogs.[40] Hobbes has recently learned how to "say hello" by placing his front paws out in front with his head lowered down towards his paws, while his back legs remain almost straight. This is similar to the yoga position of down dog, but with the head tilted back. This action gives the appearance of Hobbes bowing, as people used to do in days of old as a symbol of deference in a greeting.

As is typical of most obedience training for dogs, each of these tricks and others can be taught in approximations of the behavior, with the dog being

---

[40] Chandler (2005, 2012).

rewarded for each successive approximation of the behavior for the trick. In some cases the trick you want the therapy dog to learn can also be a natural behavior. As in the case of Hobbes learning to "say hello," you must catch the dog performing the behavior and then pair a word and hand signal with it. This action should be quickly followed with a treat or praise for the desired behavior. The therapy dog will then learn to associate the word and/or hand signal with a reward when the desired behavior is exhibited, and the dog will eventually do it on command. As you will see later in this book, these tricks are used to enhance clients' self-esteem and self-confidence, to teach social skills such as tone of voice and eye contact, to establish a sense of mastery over an object, and finally, to tolerate frustration.

Figure 8.4 Hobbes Bowing "Hello"

Another naturally occurring behavior that can be helpful to train a therapy dog to perform is to urinate or defecate on command. This training reduces stress in therapy dogs when you take them out of the office for a break. In these cases, you might only have a few minutes to allow the therapy dog to relieve him/herself. Thus, providing a command stimulus so that the dog understands that this is a time to urinate or defecate can be beneficial. So, starting from the time when my dogs are very young, whenever I see one of them urinating, I say their name and then the command "pee." Similarly, when I see one of my dogs defecating, I say the dog's name and then the command "BM" (for bowel movement). Then, when the dogs are working and we leave the working area for a break, I say their name followed by the command "pee" or "BM."

I have believed for some time that animals react to our emotional state. Many trainers have indicated that whatever a person feels while walking a dog goes straight down the leash to the dog. Thus, if I am anxious while walking my dog, the dog will detect that anxiety and react to it. I have seen Loki and sometimes Hobbes react to clients intensely by going to them, jumping up on the couch beside them, pawing them, and in some cases, which is rare for Loki, incessantly licking them. When I have asked clients to look inward to discover what is occurring at that moment, they have told me that they were starting to feel anxious or upset. Chandler has confirmed my suspicions that animals might be able to detect human emotions through their sense of smell.[41] What is it that medical alert dogs sense when they are trained to detect a seizure or

---

[41] Chandler (2012).

epilepsy? Do they smell something that humans cannot detect? That is very likely because a dog's sense of smell is far superior to the corresponding human capacity. I believe that further training can include enhancing the therapy dog's natural ability to detect and react to human emotional states. If one can train a therapy dog to go towards a person when s/he exhibits distress such as crying, this behavior can be comforting to a client. Additionally, when a therapy dog is able to detect a human emotional state, which might be outside of a person's awareness, and react to it perhaps by going over to the client and pawing or licking him/her, this behavior can allow the therapist to intervene therapeutically to help the client identify an emotional state such as disassociation. Lind's book *Animal-Assisted Therapy Activities to Motivate and Inspire* lists various tricks that dogs can learn and some of which can be aids to AAP.[42]

Certification of the Therapy Dog

Once a dog has learned basic obedience, the American Kennel Club (AKC) can assess the dog by means of the Canine Good Citizen test (CGC). The CGC test involves 10 specific skills that the dog must perform successfully. These skills include the following:

1. **Accepting a friendly stranger,** which requires that the dog allow a friendly stranger to approach and speak to the dog's human

---

[42] Lind (2009).

companion, without the dog showing any sign of offense or shyness. The dog must stay in place.

2. **Sitting politely for petting;** this requires that the dog allow a friendly stranger to pet the dog on the head and body. Again, the dog must accept the petting without offense or shyness.

3. **Appearance and grooming,** which requires that the dog accept being groomed and examined by a person other than its owner.

4. **Out for a walk (walking on a loose lead),** which requires that the dog be attentive to the human companion and respond to the person's movements and changes of direction.

5. **Walking through a crowd,** which requires that the dog and human companion can move about courteously in pedestrian traffic and that the dog be under that person's control. The dog is allowed to show some interest in strangers but should continue to walk with the person leading, without evidence of over-excitement, shyness, or offense.

6. **Sit and down on command and stay in place,** which require that the dog comply with commands to sit, go down, and remain in place until released by the person.

7. **Coming when called,** which requires that the dog come when a person calls.

8. **Reaction to another dog,** which requires that the dog can behave appropriately around other dogs.

9. **Reaction to distraction,** which requires that the dog remain calm when presented with a common distraction, such as dropping a chair. The dog may express natural interest and curiosity and/or may appear slightly startled but should stay calm, not attempt to run away, become aggressive, or bark.

10. **Supervised separation,** which requires that a dog can be left with a trusted person, if necessary, will maintain appropriate behaviors, and be able to be controlled or commanded by the trusted person.

After a dog passes the CGC test, the next step is to determine the requirements for certifying the dog as a therapy dog. Basic tasks that agencies such as Pet Partners (formerly the Delta Society), Therapy Dogs, Inc. , and Therapy Dogs International require for certifying therapy dogs include accepting a friendly stranger, being petted by strangers, walking through a crowd, reacting minimally to a distraction such as a loud noise, failing to react to an angry, yelling person, reacting minimally to being bumped from behind, being comfortable around people with crutches and/or wheelchairs, and accepting petting from several people, among other skills. For more comprehensive information regarding the U.S. agencies that certify therapy animals, please see the links listed below.

Certification for AAA or AAT can be obtained from various organizations in the U.S., including Pet Partners, Therapy Dogs, Inc., and Therapy Dogs International, or Saint John Ambulance Therapy Dogs in

Canada, and others.[43] However, it should be noted that for a professional to utilize AAP, certification of the dog as a therapy dog is not required by federal or state law or by professional licensing boards. Nevertheless, I believe that having a dog certified as a therapy dog ameliorates clients' concerns about the dog and is a prudent risk- and liability-minimization strategy.

Agencies that provide certification for therapy animals in the U.S. include the following:

Pet Partners – formerly the Delta Society
875 124th Ave NE #101
Bellevue, Washington 98005
Phone: (425) 679-5500
Fax: (425) 679-5539
Email: info@petpartners.org
Website: http://www.petpartners.org

Therapy Dogs International, Inc.
88 Bartley Road
Flanders, New Jersey 07836
Phone: (973) 252-9800
Fax: (973) 252-71717
E-mail: tdi@gti.net
Website: http://www.tdi-dog.org/

Therapy Dogs, INC.
P.O. Box 20227
Cheyenne, Wyoming 82003

---

[43] Butler (2004); Burch (1996); Chandler (2005, 2012); Eggiman (2006); Fine (2010); Matuszek (2010); Minatrea and Wesley (2008); Parshall (2003); Wilkes (2009).

Phone: (877) 843-7364
Phone: (307) 432-0272
FAX: (307) 638-2079
Email: therapydogsinc@qwestoffice.net
Website: http://www.therapydogs.com/.

Chapter
9

Theoretical Orientations that can be Applied with Animal-Assisted Psychotherapy

According to Chandler et al., successful therapeutic outcomes can be attributed in part to a therapist's theoretical orientation.[1] Hence, it is prudent to discuss how combining animal-assisted psychotherapy (AAP) with particular theoretical orientations can be helpful for therapists' specific practices. Other authors also suggest that when a therapist does not have a specific framework of practice, any interventions would be arbitrary and might not be beneficial.[2] Moreover, Chandler states that those who do not fully understand the various ways that AAP can benefit and enhance psychotherapy would not be able to take full advantage of AAP.[3] Thus, if one does not understand how AAP can benefit psychotherapy, one might also not understand how AAP fits with particular theoretical

---

[1] Chandler et al. (2010).

[2] Teyber (2000).

[3] Chandler (2012).

orientations. To incorporate AAP into a therapy session, therapists must assess how animal-assisted interventions can meet the needs of a client and how they can frame those interventions from their respective orientations. In addition, therapists need to use their theoretical orientations and their understanding of AAP to develop appropriate treatment goals. When these factors are combined, AAP becomes a method utilized in counseling that can facilitate additional progress for clients.[4]

The following sections demonstrate how AAP can be implemented with some of the orientations therapists use in their work.

Cognitive Orientation

Cognitive therapy (CT) was developed by Aaron T. Beck and is considered the precursor to cognitive behavioral therapy (CBT; see later in this chapter). A therapist working in a CT orientation seeks to help clients overcome difficulties by identifying and changing cognitions or cognitive processes. This orientation involves helping clients to develop skills for modifying beliefs and identifying distorted thinking. A cognitively oriented therapy treatment is collaborative and typically consists of therapists testing patients' assumptions and identifying how their thoughts are distorted, unrealistic, and unhelpful and then challenging these distorted or unhelpful beliefs and thoughts. A particular area of interest for cognitively

---

[4] Chandler (2012).

oriented therapists is the schemas by which clients function. Core schemas are the fundamental levels at which our beliefs, attitudes, rules, and assumptions about the self, others, and how the world develops and influences our perception of our experiences. Specific techniques that cognitively oriented therapists might use include disrupting irrational thoughts and/or clients practicing alternative thoughts to the irrational ones.[5]

When an individual's core schemas are rigid and extreme, as is often the case for someone who has experienced a significant trauma in childhood, it is often difficult for the person to assimilate or accommodate information that challenges their schemas. Assimilation is the incorporation of new concepts into existing schemas, whereas accommodation is the process by which existing schemas are modified to adapt to the new information or experience. As an example of assimilation, when a person sees an unfamiliar dog, the person will likely assimilate the animal into his/her dog schema. As an example of accommodation, if a client has a core schema that "all dogs are bad," the person might modify this schema after meeting many dogs who have behaved well toward him/her so that the schema becomes "some dogs are bad" or "the dog that attacked me was a bad dog." In this way, the core schema becomes less rigid and less extreme.

AAP can be beneficial in challenging a person's core schemas and irrational thoughts. For example, clients whose core schema is that they are unlovable and that no one likes them might state that my furry facilitator does not like them. Here, the presence of the furry facilitator has

---

[5] Fine (2010); Garfield and Bergin (1986); Mahoney (1991); Price (2007).

activated a core schema, which the therapist can then challenge. Had the animal co-therapist not been present, this core schema might not have presented itself; thus, the therapy dog assists in illuminating clients' inner processes.

For examples of how AAP works with the cognitive orientation, see the stories of Richard in Chapter 11 and Coco in Chapter 12.

Behavioral Orientation

According to Garfield and Bergin, there are four schools of behavioral therapists: The first school views behaviors and therefore behavior therapy as an application of a theory of learning.[6] A second behavioral therapy school considers mediational factors, such as thoughts and feelings that impact behaviors. The third school is referred to as "technical eclecticism," and these therapists use whatever techniques work. The last school of behavioral therapists does not necessarily follow a particular theory but works from an experimental-clinical method.[7]

Behavioral therapists' main focus is to improve the quality of clients' lives, which they accomplish by developing goals focused on altering behaviors that impede clients' social, occupational, and other important activities.[8] The main role of the therapist is to teach clients new skills

---

[6] Garfield and Bergin (1986).

[7] Ibid.

[8] Garfield and Bergin (1986); Chandler (2012); Chandler and Mahoney (1991); Portrie-Bethke, Minton, Fernando, and O'Callaghan (2010).

through instruction, modeling, and rehearsal of desired behaviors.

AAP therefore appears to be a good adjunct to behavioral therapists in that therapy dogs can help clients to practice and successfully acquire new behaviors. The therapist and therapy dog can be pivotal in modeling appropriate social behaviors. Nevertheless, for behavioral therapy to be successful, a client must be willing and motivated to change.[9] An animal-assisted intervention that I have often used to demonstrate to clients the capacity for self-discipline and impulse control is to have Loki, my collie mix furry facilitator, lie on the floor, be told to wait, have several treats placed around him in the room, some as close as a few inches from his mouth, and have him remain in this position until he hears the release word that allows him to stand and have his rewards. Young clients are often truly amazed by Loki's self-control, as they are well aware that Loki is a dog that "lives to eat."

For examples of how AAP works with the behavioral orientation, see the stories of David, Crystal, and Susan in Chapter 11 and those of Mandy and Peter in Chapter 12.

Cognitive-Behavioral Orientation

When therapists works from a cognitive behavioral therapy (CBT) orientation, they focus on three areas: 1) thoughts, 2) feelings, and 3) behaviors. This orientation is not

---

[9] Chandler (2012); Chandler et al. (2010).

concerned with the root cause of problems but only with a client's present-day functioning.

The primary goal of therapists practicing CBT is to identify and challenge the client's irrational beliefs that influence maladaptive feelings and behaviors. CBT is a directive approach, and the therapist is therefore viewed as a teacher or practice partner who helps clients to challenge their dysfunctional beliefs, thoughts, and behaviors. This approach then helps clients to learn new and assimilated ways of believing, feeling, and behaving.[10] Some of the originators of CBT, such as Aaron Beck, indicate that rapport and trust in the therapist-client relationship is important, whereas other CBT authors, such as Albert Ellis, do not believe that rapport and trust are necessary.[11]

According to Chandler and other authors, CBT can be utilized with AAP, as I often use it, by asking clients to get a therapy dog to perform a trick.[12] If clients are unable to get the therapy dog to perform the trick and give up, we then explore why they gave up, explore their frustration, negative thinking, and other behaviors or thoughts they could try to be successful. For example, I noted that a client often reached out and tried to pet or call one of my therapy dogs to him. On several occasions, the therapy dog ignored him, and so he stopped reaching his hand out and calling the therapy dog. Given that this client had a tendency to lack assertiveness and did not express his true wants, needs, and expectations, this opportunity provided a less threatening avenue to explore his verbal and non-verbal

---

[10] Chandler (2012); Garfield and Bergin (1986); McWilliams (1999); Mahoney (1991).

[11] Chandler (2012).

[12] Chandler (2005, 2012); Chandler et al. (2010); Fine (2010).

behaviors, his tendency to expect that this need would not be met, and his tendency to give up, and it provided a way to practice skills and behaviors that would likely result in his needs being met. Thus, clients can also be encouraged to practice certain social skills with the therapy dog and to practice positive behaviors that they have been struggling with in their life.[13]

Therapists may also model specific behaviors with the therapy dog, and clients may also be asked to practice new and more useful behaviors that can benefit them socially. Having a client successfully interact with a therapy dog can enhance the client's self-confidence. Moreover, practicing new, positive behaviors with the therapy dog is more fun and less threatening to the client, than practicing a new behavior without the interaction of a therapy dog. Additionally, the therapist's feedback on constructive client-therapy dog interactions can support clients to adopt pro-social behaviors.[14]

We can also use AAP with CBT in a less directive manner. For example, if a client were to innocently comment, "He (the therapy dog) doesn't like me?" A CBT therapist might respond with, "what is he doing that tells you he does not like you?" Such an interaction would provide an opportunity to challenge any irrational thoughts that clients have about themselves.

AAP along with CBT can also be used to help clients learn socially appropriate interactions and the causes and effects of their behavior. Therapy animals tend to provide immediate and honest feedback through their

---

[13] Chandler (2012).

[14] Chandler et al. (2010).

responses to both positive and negative behaviors, which can immediately be fed back to clients in vivo so that work on their own behaviors can be accomplished.[15] Clients can also perceive the therapy animal's reaction as less threatening to their psyche because they see the animal as non-judgmental.

For examples of how AAP works with the cognitive-behavioral orientation, see the stories of Mark, David, Brittany, Susan, and Crystal in Chapter 11, those of Mandy and Peter in Chapter 12, those of Deborah, Tiffany, and Rachel in Chapter 13, and the second family vignette in Chapter 14.

Person- or Client-Centered Orientation

Person- or client-centered theory (PCT) was developed by Carl Rogers. Fine reports that therapists whose orientation is based on PCT can use AAP.[16] PCT is typically considered a nondirective approach in which the therapist observes the client's experiences and then explores the potential meaning and results of those experiences. Goals of PCT include assisting clients with self-acceptance, reflecting and clarifying their verbal and non-verbal communications, and enhancing their insights. These goals are primarily achieved through the therapist's unconditional positive regard for the

---

[15] Chandler (2012); Fine (2010).
[16] Fine (2010).

client and by providing a safe therapeutic environment in which the client can feel safety, comfort, and trust towards themselves and others. PCT therapists do not direct a session and do not assume responsibility for the client. Instead, the therapist fosters safety for the client by being consistent, authentic, genuine, kind, accepting, warm, and compassionate.[17] When using PCT and AAP, therapists might reflect on their observations of the client-therapy dog interactions and explore what this means to the client. As stated, because the therapy dog is non-judgmental, accepting, and caring towards clients, the furry facilitator helps to facilitate a safe therapeutic environment that can encourage clients to share their experiences and therefore develop insight.[18]

One of Rogers's central tenets for this orientation is that the therapist must demonstrate unconditional positive regard so that clients can progressively trust themselves and move toward becoming more self-actualized. AAP can facilitate this experience as therapy dogs accept unconditionally and are genuine in their reactions.[19]

In PCT, the therapist-client relationship and the therapeutic atmosphere are considered primary mediums for healing; therefore, any animal-assisted interventions that foster a safe place and a safe relationship would be beneficial. One of the ways I can facilitate a safe relationship between the client and therapist is by allowing the client-therapy dog relationship to exist. When a client enters my

---

[17] Chandler (2012); Chandler et al. (2010); Glickauf-Hughes and Wells (2007).

[18] Chandler (2012).

[19] Chandler (et al. 2010); Fine (2010); Matuszek (2010).

office, the therapy dog walks to greet the person, often wagging his/her tail, and then follows the client back to his/her seat. Next, there are usually several minutes in which the client and therapy dog "say hello," which I do not interrupt. Only when the client breaks the contact with the therapy dog do I then engage with the client.

Many of the stories in the following chapters demonstrate the PCT orientation, such as when the therapy dogs show unconditional love and acceptance, the therapist allows clients the necessary time to get to know the therapy dog, allows the client and therapy dog to say hello and good-bye, and when clients reach for the dog for comfort, and the therapist reflects this behavior.[20]

Solution-Focused Brief Therapy Orientation

The solution-focused therapist sees clients as competent and focused on what is possible. The main goal of solution-focused brief therapy (SFBT) is to shift the client from focusing on problems to solutions. In SFBT, clients are reassured to believe that positive changes are possible. SFBT therapists ask clients to identify that which is going right in their lives and what needs to happen to make their lives better. Clients are then encouraged to determine what actions they can take to make this occur. As with other orientations, the quality of the relationship between the

---

[20] Fine (2010); Wilkes (2009).

therapist and client is a determining factor in the outcome of SFBT. Once clients achieve satisfactory, life-enhancing solutions to their current problems, the therapy is terminated.[21]

Fine reports that therapists whose orientation is SFBT can successfully use AAP.[22] He reports that SFBT and AAP provide an environment in which clients can practice new behaviors that enhance self- confidence.

In addition, according to Pichot, basic principles of SFBT include the following: If something works, don't change it, or do more of it; if something doesn't work, do something different; solutions might not relate to the actual problem; small steps can lead to large changes; we negotiate and create our own future; no problem is persistent, and exceptions can exist.[23]

A particular technique of SFBT is known as the miracle question. According to SFBT therapists, the miracle question consists of five components and might sound something like this: "When you leave this session today, you will likely go home and continue on with your typical activities. Eventually, you will go to bed and fall asleep. However, during the night a miracle occurs, and the problem that brought you here today is resolved. This happens while you are sleeping, which means you are not aware that the miracle has occurred. When you wake up in the morning, what is it that you might notice, a small change that helps you know that the problem is gone and the miracle has occurred?" When an SFBT therapist uses the miracle question in conjunction with AAP, the therapist

---

[21] Chandler (2012); Chandler et al. (2010); Pichot (2012).

[22] Fine (2010).

[23] Pichot (2012).

would likely ask something like, "I wonder what Loki would notice about you that would be different the next time we meet, after the miracle had happened? What would he see or hear differently about you?" It is important that the miracle question contain all five components for it to be fruitful. The first component is that of a significant change. The second component is that a miracle occurs, and the problem is no longer present. The third component is that of immediacy. The fourth component is that of surprise, such that the person is unaware that the problem has been resolved. The last component is that the person notices some small detail indicating that the miracle has occurred.[24]

SFBT and AAP appear to be a good combination for clients. As stated, the therapy dog can be instrumental in practicing new skills and devising new solutions. When a person lacks assertiveness, for instance, we can utilize the therapy dog to help him/her practice assertiveness skills and gain the cooperation of the therapy dog, which can enhance self-esteem and confidence.

In SFBT and AAP, the therapy dog can help to model relationship skills by prompting discussions of the client-therapy dog interactions or the therapist-therapy dog interactions.[25] Additionally, when utilizing SFBT and AAP, we can help clients to develop social skills, such as appropriate non-verbal behaviors that the client has thus far been unable to acquire. When these skills are achieved, we see an increase in self-confidence, especially when clients transfer these newly acquired skills to their lives.

---

[24] Ibid.
[25] Chandler et al. (2010).

According to Pichot, SFBT and AAP share common values.[26] These values include respecting life, change, people's unique perspectives, the wisdom of the client or therapy animal, goal-oriented interventions, the alliance among the client, therapist, and therapy animal as an important aspect of change, and the idea that a small change can make an important difference in an individual's life.

For examples of how AAP works with the solution-focused brief therapy orientation, see the stories of David, Crystal, and Richard in Chapter 11 and the story of Peter in Chapter 12.

Play Therapy Orientation

Play therapy is defined as an interpersonal process using the therapeutic influence of play to resolve or help develop optimal growth or to prevent psychosocial issues.[27] Play is considered the language of children. and a way of working through emotional difficulties, as children have not yet developed the cognitive and verbal skills to process these difficulties.[28] Hence, a good play therapist should enjoy interacting with children and playing and should be able to set clear, firm boundaries while being adaptable and imaginative. Additionally, a good play therapist should be

---

[26] Pichot (2012).

[27] Fine (2001).

[28] Kaduson and Schaefer (2000); McNally (2001); Parish-Plass (2008, 2013).

able to recognize the feelings that a child is expressing and should provide appropriate age-level interpretations. Unconditional acceptance of the child, one of Rogers's tenets for therapy, is paramount in play therapy. At all times, the play therapist should maintain a profound respect for the child's ability to solve his/her own problems, allow the child to lead the process, and should not rush the therapy process.[29]

Play therapy can consist of four phases. The first phase is called the introductory phase, in which a child begins to develop a relationship with the therapist. If the child's previous experiences have been abusive or neglectful, then developing trust can take some time. The second phase is the exploratory space in which the child begins to develop some self-awareness and reveals inner conflicts. The third phase is the consolidating phase, in which the child begins to create lasting growth and to repair that which has hurt him or her. The last phase is the termination phase, which involves slowly tapering sessions and allows the relationship with the therapist to become less important to the child.[30]

According to some authors, children who experienced abuse and/or neglect during the preverbal stage of development might exhibit difficulty with symbolization. This difficulty might present problems within play therapy, which is a preferred therapy method with children and often depends on symbolization to reach the child's inner world.[31] Nevertheless, this difficulty can be overcome with the presence of a well-trained, who can

---

[29] Kaduson and Schaefer (2000); McNally (2001).
[30] Kaduson and Schaefer (2000).
[31] Parish-Plass (2008).

spontaneously provide symbolism of the human-human dynamic, which can help children to illuminate their abuse in a safer and less threatening manner because they can project their experiences onto their interactions with the therapy dog.

Figure 9.1 Zoey: in training as a therapy dog

Play therapy comes in many shapes and forms, such as cognitive-behavioral, short-term Gestalt, child-centered, short-term solution-oriented, and family play therapy.[32] Cognitive-behavioral play therapy (CBPT) is intended particularly for preschool and early elementary aged children. CBPT focuses mainly on issues related to control, mastery, and accountability for changing one's own behavior. A CBPT therapist assists in developing a child's self-control, sense of accomplishment, and adaptive ways of coping. CBPT can be either directive or non-directive. Some of the techniques used in CBPT include the therapist's use of hero images to evoke pride, affection, and assertiveness. The term for this technique is called emotive imagery. A CBPT therapist might also employ contingency

---

[32] Ibid.

management techniques, such as positive reinforcement and shaping or differential reinforcement of other behaviors.[33]

According to Parish-Plass, play therapy allows children to communicate their experiences, emotions, and inner worlds through Winnicott's idea of "potential space."[34] This potential space is a complicated linking of children's outer and inner worlds, where reality and fantasy contribute to children's feelings, thoughts, perceptions, and understanding of the world and themselves. Parish-Plass states that play therapy allows for this potential space to be present and provides a safe psychological distance so that children can process and explore any difficult or threatening experiences.[35]

Play therapy can be directive and non-directive.[36] When play therapy is utilized with AAP, the therapy dog becomes part of the play, so that the therapist might ask the child to get the dog to perform a trick or to teach the dog a new trick. The goals of canine-assisted play therapy (CAPT) include learning to attach, developing empathy, self-regulation, problem solving, and developing self-efficacy.[37]

Animals, particularly dogs, are naturally playful creatures. Dogs naturally enjoy the game of chase and catch, seeking objects, fetching objects, playing tug of war, and roughhousing. Many of these playful activities enjoyed by dogs can be utilized in a therapeutic manner. Therefore, play therapy and AAP can be beneficial for clients.

---

[33] Fine (2010); Kaduson and Schaefer (2000).
[34] Parish-Plass (2013).
[35] Ibid.
[36] Fine (2010); Kaduson and Schaefer (2000).
[37] Fine (2010).

The stories of Mark, David, Crystal, Susan, and Richard in Chapter 11 illustrate some of the goals described above.

Attachment Theory Orientation

According to many writers, theorists, and therapists, attachment theory suggests that humans have an instinctual need to protect, to be protected, and to be emotionally attached to others. These authors suggest that any behavior engaged in maintaining or gaining closeness to another who is perceived as being more able to cope with the circumstance would be considered an attachment behavior.[38] Some of these authors have also suggested that the human-animal relationship can parallel the human-human relationship. Specifically, pets or therapy animals can provide unconditional love, acceptance, comfort, and support in times of need.[39] These authors also posit that in treating clients with attachment issues, the therapist would be greatly concerned with defense mechanisms, transference, shame, guilt, and anxiety.

According to Bowlby, infants demonstrate attachment behaviors from birth.[40] One such behavior is

---

[38] Bowlby (1982); Fine (2010); Garfield and Bergin (1986); Goldstein (1995); Johnson (2004); Mahoney (1991); Levenson (1995); Parish-Plass (2013); Wilkes (2009); Zilcha-Mano, Mikulincer, and Shaver (2011).

[39] Chandler (2012); Fine (2010); Wilkes (2009); Zilcha-Mano, Mikulincer, and Shaver (2011).

[40] Bowlby (1982).

that of clinging or reaching for physical contact. Bowlby also indicates that babies appear to be comforted by certain social interactions, such as being picked up, spoken to, and being caressed.[41] Another behavior that babies exhibit related to attachment is that of smiling and making noises. As evidence of these attachment behaviors, Bowlby describes situations in which children separated from their mother might suck their thumb or eat food. He states that these behaviors indicate that perhaps the thumb and food represent the mother and that the children are attempting to soothe themselves by engaging in these attachment behaviors. These behaviors are instinctual and motivated towards attachment and self-preservation. Bowlby states that when infants are securely attached, they are more likely to seek others and will engage in social behaviors promoting attachment with others in their environment. In contrast, an infant that is insecurely attached will often not seek others or will not engage in social behaviors encouraging attaching with them.[42]

Moreover, Bowlby states that infants often show attachment behaviors towards inanimate objects, such as feeding bottles, pieces of cloth, a blanket, or a cuddly toy. He postulates that these objects are a replacement object for the mother, as they typically will comfort the child when a mother is not present. Thus, it seems plausible that infants and people could therefore seek the attachment of a pet or therapy dog to provide comfort in times of stress. These

---

[41] Ibid.
[42] Ibid.

objects would be considered transitional objects as defined by Winnicott.[43]

According to Johnson, there are 10 central principles of attachment theory.[44] First, attachment is an instinctual activating force. Thus, seeking and maintaining connections with others is an important drive for all humans. Second, autonomy is complimented by a secure dependence. In other words, we can only be autonomous when we have a secure dependence. Third, our sense of attachment provides a critical safe haven. Therefore, our innate survival depends on healthy attachment to others. Fourth, our sense of attachment affords us a secure base from which to explore self, others, and our experiences. Fifth, access and responsiveness to emotions help to build bonds of attachment. Sixth, attachment needs are activated when fear and uncertainty are present. Seventh, the course of separation distress is foreseeable. It is likely that even those to whom we see who are securely attached, can feel separation distress when they are unable, for whatever reason, to feel their emotional attachment to others. Eighth, there are two main insecure forms of attachment, anxious and avoidant. Ninth, working models of the self and others define our attachment style. Finally, tenth, seclusion and loss are fundamentally traumatizing.[45]

Wilkes states that she believes she learned how to attach through her relationship with her pet dogs and not with her human family, who were dysfunctional and abusive.[46] Fine agrees with Wilkes that animals can foster

---

[43] Ibid.

[44] Johnson (2004).

[45] Johnson (2004).

[46] Wilkes (2009).

the attachment of a person as well as acceptance of the self by offering reassurance, calmness, and a sense of security.[47] Wilkes further states that in some cases, clients who have difficulty attaching to animals also have difficulty attaching to humans.[48] Similarly, Zilcha-Mano, Mikulincer, and Shaver found a positive correlation between a person's attachment style with people and with animals.[49] In other words, if people were anxiously attached to humans, they would be similarly anxiously attached to animals.

Many researchers and treatment providers have concluded that child victims of severe abuse and/or neglect often suffer from insecure attachment and will typically use defenses that, although helpful in their survival of the abuse and/or neglect, become maladaptive in other situations with children and adults. In some cases, these children often have a diminished capacity to empathize with others. Without intervention, this problem can result in the child's growing into adulthood and engaging in inappropriate and unhealthy relationships with others. Attachment-oriented therapists seek to assist these clients with emotional expression leading to insight, change, and increased quality of life and to increase the likelihood that these individuals can develop healthy attachment behaviors. AAP can address these issues, provides opportunities for thwarting them, and provides additional tools for enlightening the client's inner world.[50]

---

[47] Fine (2010).

[48] Wilkes (2009).

[49] Zilcha-Mano, Mikulincer, and Shaver (2011).

[50] Parish-Plass (2008).

Fine posits that AAP may enhance attachment and help clients to see themselves as likeable.[51] When the therapy dog reacts promptly and in a caring way to a child, this can foster attachment. In addition, children and adults often anthropomorphize animals and will exclaim, "Hobbes likes me," thus stating that they are likeable. This can be a powerful antidote for a person who has suffered negative attachments with caregivers or been told over and over again that they are unlikeable. Fine also posits that animals can serve as attachment figures and as transitional objects (see the section on object relations orientation below).

For examples of how AAP works with the attachment theory orientation, see the stories of Mark, Susan, and Richard in Chapter 11, those of Mandy and Coco in Chapter 12, those of Christine, Tiffany, and Rachel in Chapter 13, and the first family vignette in Chapter 14.

Object Relations Orientation

Several authors note that contributors to object relations theory include Klein, Fairburn, Winnicott, and Balint for the American school, and the British contributions to object relations theory include Kernberg, Loewald, and Kohut, among others. According to these authors, the main drive of humans is to establish and relate to others, and through the establishment of these relationships, the view of the self develops and is then continued into existing and

---

[51] Fine (2010).

future relationships. The process by which the development of the self occurs is referred to as "internalization." Thus, "objects" can be external (the "real" person/thing/animal) and internal mental images of previously encountered external objects. Furthermore, "objects" can be people, things, animals, or a fantasy and can also be internalized as good, bad, anxious, calm, gratifying, exciting, or rejecting. According to these authors, this theory postulates that people's motivations are for relationships, not necessarily for pleasure or aggression (as other psychodynamic or analytic theories postulate), that these relationships may be based on the mental representation of the early child-caretaker relationship, and that these patterns of relating become enduring for people.[52]

A term that will be very familiar to object relations therapists is that of the "transitional object." The definition of transitional object can be accredited to Winnicott and is defined as an object that creates a place of comfort and safety between the internal and external worlds.[53]

A few authors, speaking of Winnicott's concepts regarding object relations theory, have posited that companion animals can be viewed as a transitional object. This transitional object provides safety so that a child may separate from the dependent relationship with a caretaker to develop independence. These authors also posit that animals can be transitional objects for adults and that, more important, animals can be viewed as transitional beings because the animal, like humans, can show intentional

---

[52] Fine (2010); Glickauf-Hughes and Wells (2007); Goldstein (1995); Levenson (1995); Mahoney (1991); Moore and Fine (1990); Parish-Plass (2013); Sacks (2008); Teyber (2000); Wilkes (2009).
[53] Glickauf-Hughes and Wells (2007); Goldstein (1995); Wilkes (2009).

behaviors.[54] Thus, it seems likely that the therapy dog can serve as a transitional object that allows the client to take subjective phenomena and bring them into the real world.

This transitional object can symbolize the "good-enough mother" and is used during times of separation or stress. Winnicott is also credited with defining the terms "good-enough mother" and "holding." A good-enough mother is an external object that provides the appropriate amount of constancy and comfort to the infant, and in turn, the good enough mother creates the "holding." This holding refers to containing the emotions for the child, such as emotions, insecurities, and/or frustrations. According to some authors, when people do not have a good-enough mother, they cannot achieve emotional maturity.[55]

In addition, the "mother" has a special purpose, which is to be empathic towards her infant and to be there to receive spontaneous signals, which become the source of the "True Self." When the infant's needs are met repeatedly, the sense of the self as being worthy, good, wanted, worthwhile, and lovable can develop – this is the "True Self." The origin of the "True Self" cannot become an actuality without the mother's empathic responses. If the mother is not good enough and she repeatedly fails to meet the infant's needs or substitutes her own needs, this behavior can lead to the development of acquiescence by the infant. This self-protective acquiescence on the infant's part becomes the earliest stage of the "False Self." A compliant "False Self" reacts to environmental demands as

---

[54] Chandler (2005); Fine (2010); Glickauf-Hughes and Wells (2007); Parish-Plass (2013); Wilkes (2009).

[55] Glickauf-Hughes and Wells (2007); Sacks (2008); Zilcha-Mano, Mikulincer, and Shaver (2011).

a solution to hide the "True Self." The "False Self" defense can range from being polite, socially adaptable, or to the truly split-off compliant self in which the child attempts to be "perfect." This behavior can lead infants and, later, children, adolescents, and adults to believe consciously or more likely unconsciously that they are unworthy, unlovable, not good enough, and unwanted.[56]

Wilkes also posits that companion animals can foster a sense of worthiness, attachment, can act as "silent" therapists and as a "good-enough mother," and can help to teach calming or grounding skills. When animals act as a good-enough mother, they provide the transitional space for risk, exploration, and discovery for healthy growth. According to Wilkes, clients who were unable to establish an attachment with therapy animals also had difficulty attaching to humans. [57]

Thus, AAP can provide the necessary conditions for clients to risk, explore, and discover when the therapy dog and therapist are a good-enough mother and can create the necessary holding environment for the safe validation of their experiences.[58] Finally, and perhaps most important, AAP can enhance the development of the client's trust toward the therapist.[59] This trust is of paramount importance in work with persons abused in childhood because without trust no work can be accomplished.

In therapy, one of the object relations therapist's major roles, which the therapy dog can assist, is to create a safe holding environment that is simultaneously supportive

---

[56] Sacks (2008); Wells, Glickauf-Hughes, and Beaudoin (1995).
[57] Wilkes (2009).
[58] Ibid.
[59] Ibid.

and questioning. The therapists' holding will include empathy, a voice laden with compassion, a sense of steadiness, and a sense that the therapist will be there and can tolerate what is being shared.[60]

Fine posits that AAP may enhance self-object experiences such as attachment or the likeability of the self. Moreover, children and adults often anthropomorphize animals and will exclaim, "Loki likes me," thus stating that they are likeable.

Sacks agrees that object relations therapy and AAP can be combined and will be helpful to clients.[61] Specifically, clients can benefit from the attention from a therapy dog and the freedom to give affection and "devotion" to the dog. Thus, it seems that a corrective emotional experience with a new object might occur, i.e., when the therapy dog is empathic, responsive, and loving, this behavior might provide an opportunity for the "True Self" to emerge. Moreover, for clients with intimacy issues who are unable to establish a relationship with a significant other and find themselves alone and lonely, the therapy dog can be touched and gives unconditional love and acceptance, which can allay some of the loneliness experienced by clients. A therapist cannot necessarily gratify these physical needs and desires. The therapy dog might also be a facilitating influence for inhibited and constricted clients who find it agonizing to relate verbally to the human therapist. Pressure to do so can be lessened when a therapy

---

[60] Fine (2010); Moore and Fine (1990); Sacks (2008); Wilkes (2009); Zilcha-Mano, Mikulincer, and Shaver (2011).
[61] Sacks (2008).

dog is present as s/he can be a neutral talking point for the client.[62]

For examples of how object relations therapy works with AAP, see the stories of Brittany and David in Chapter 11, those of Mandy, Peter, and Coco in Chapter 12, those of Melanie, Tiffany, and Rachel in Chapter 13, and the first family vignette in Chapter 14.

Psychodynamic Orientation

According to some authors, psychodynamic therapists believe that conscious and unconscious forces motivate clients' behaviors and attitudes. Thus, a psychodynamically oriented therapist might focus on the client's relationship experiences and bring to light unconscious motivations for their behaviors.[63] Thus, having a therapy animal in the room creates another relationship about which clients can process their experiences. Additionally, according to Chandler and Parish-Plass, in a traditional therapy setting, there are two relationships in the room: the client's relationship to the therapist and the therapist's relationship to the client.[64] Hence, when we add the presence of a therapy animal, we now have a few more relationships to help explore the client's experiences: the two relationships already mentioned plus the client's relationship to the therapy animal, the therapy animal's relationship to the client, the

---

[62] Ibid.

[63] Chandler (2012); Goldstein (1995).

[64] Chandler (2012); Parish-Plass (2013).

therapist's relationship to the therapy animal, and the therapy animal's relationship to the therapist.

One of the roles of the psychodynamic therapist is to recognize and process the relational dynamics of clients so that they can become more aware of themselves in relation to others. During this process, clients can see the therapist as a transitional object; similarly, clients can see the therapy dog as a transitional object if they were to project their experience onto the therapy dog.[65] In some cases therapy dogs might be better transitional objects than the therapist, partly because clients understand that humans might judge and respond to them in ways unrelated to the clients, whereas a therapy dog responds quickly, genuinely, and nonjudgmentally. For example, if a client were to become angry, raise his or her voice, and use other non-verbal behaviors indicating anger, the therapy dog might respond quickly by moving away from the client. Such is the case with my therapy dog Loki, who is uncomfortable with expressions of anger in the aforementioned ways. When he has been sitting with a client who has expressed anger by raising his or her voice and/or waving arms aggressively, he will immediately get down from where he is sitting near the client and go to his safe spot in my office or come to me for protection. This can help the therapist to immediately intervene in a therapeutic manner and allow the therapy process to be enhanced. Nonetheless, as in many situations that I have experienced, because a therapy dog has a prior relationship with clients that is typically based on mutual acceptance and positive connection, both clients and

---

[65] Chandler (2012).

therapy dog quickly move through this disconnection to regain the connection they once had.

Additionally, when working in a psychodynamic orientation, a therapist may be well aware when a client is projecting onto the therapist or in some cases onto the therapy dog. Many authors have conceptualized "projection" as a mental process in which an unacceptable impulse or idea that belongs to the self is then ascribed to the external world.[66] This behavior is considered a defense mechanism.

Another defensive mechanism, according to psychodynamic therapists, is that of "transference." Transference is considered to be a displacement of feelings, thoughts, and/or behaviors, originally experienced in relation to a significant figure during childhood, onto a person with whom they are currently in a relationship. Therapists often encounter the defense mechanism of transference. Any transference interpretation is best made in a concrete and detailed manner so that clients can recognize for themselves what the therapist is stating.[67] In contrast, some authors currently consider countertransference to be the therapist's awareness of or empathetic reactions to the client's interpersonal dynamics.[68]

Psychodynamically oriented therapists would also be likely to observe another defense mechanism, that of

---

[66] Glickauf-Hughes and Wells (2007); Goldstein (1995); Moore and Fine (1990); Parish-Plass (2013); Zilcha-Mano, Mikulincer, and Shaver (2011).

[67] Glickauf-Hughes and Wells (2007); Goldstein (1995); Levenson (1995); Moore and Fine (1990); McWilliams (1999); Parish-Plass (2013).

[68] Goldstein (1995); Levenson (1995).

"splitting" or "all or none" thinking. Splitting refers to a person's tendency to categorize thoughts, emotions, relationships, and so forth, on either end of a differentiated scale. Splitting can also indicate the failure in a person's thinking to bring together both positive and negative qualities of the self and others into a unified, realistic whole; for example, "everybody hates me." Splitting allows any possibly objectionable thought to be identified and subsequently denied from conscious awareness in a maladaptive attempt to protect the "self" (i.e., the ego, for the purposes of this description) from upsetting material.[69]

AAP can facilitate a psychodynamic orientation process in that people often relate to the furry facilitator as if s/he were another person. I have seen my clients talk to the dog co-therapist and reach out to the therapy dog when they are seeking comfort. Simply the presence of the therapy dog can elicit subconscious thoughts and feelings, as you will see in the vignettes of David in Chapter 11, Coco in Chapter 12, Christine, Tiffany, and Rachel in Chapter 13, and both family vignettes in Chapter 14.

Interpersonal Process Orientation

A therapist who works from an interpersonal process orientation integrates three different theories. These theories are interpersonal theory, originally developed by Harry Stack Sullivan, object relations theory, as discussed above, and family systems theory. Interpersonal theory

---

[69] Price (2007); Wells, Glickauf-Hughes, and Beaudoin (1995).

stipulates that anxiety in interpersonal relationships is the central motivation for all human behavior and that humans make elaborate attempts to avoid and minimize this anxiety to avoid "derogation and rejection" by others or even by the self, and the interpersonal therapist believes that these personality characteristics develop due to repetitive interactions with parents or caretakers.[70] Object relations theory has already been outlined above.

The last theory that is integrated into the interpersonal process orientation is the family systems theory. Original contributors to the family systems theory include Gregory Bateson, Virginia Satir, Jay Hayley, and others. Family systems theory posits that children are scripted into familiar roles such as the "responsible or good child, problem/bad child, hero, rescuer or invisible child." An interpersonal process therapist's main goal is to help clients adjust to the good and bad in their families, in other words, to accept themselves, including their faults and their strengths. Thus, the basic tenets of an interpersonal process therapist are that problems are interpersonal in nature, the most important source of learning about the self and others is our early familial experiences, and the therapeutic relationship is the most important opportunity for change in the client.[71] For an interpersonal process therapist, it is important that clients experience the same types of issues with the therapist that they experience in real life, such as control, power, and mistrust. The idea is that with the therapist, clients can resolve these old issues and find new ways of relating that enhance their lives.

---

[70] Teyber (2000).
[71] Levenson (1995); Teyber (2000).

Given that the therapeutic relationship is central to the process of change in the interpersonal process orientation, one can easily see how AAP can be beneficial. As mentioned above, therapy dogs are known to help with rapport building, provide unconditional acceptance and comfort, and they typically react immediately to the client's process and emotions. Moreover, with the therapy dog engaged in the therapeutic change process, we have more relational dynamics than would typically occur in a therapist-client dynamic.

Many of the vignettes in subsequent chapters portray aspects of the interpersonal process orientation, including the many facets of the relationships between the client and therapist, the client and the therapy dog, and the therapist and the therapy dog. The vignettes also demonstrate some of the ascribed roles that the client, therapist, and therapy dog portray or embody in the therapy process.

Emotionally Focused Orientation

Emotionally focused therapy (EFT) was developed by Susan Johnson. EFT is primarily based on attachment theory but also includes aspects of person-centered, constructivist, and systems theories. As its name implies, emotionally focused therapy is based on emotions. EFT for couples is a short-term therapy, often lasting eight to 20 sessions.[72]

A therapist working in the emotionally focused orientation proposes that emotions are innately adaptive and, when activated, can help clients change difficult emotional states or undesirable self-experiences. An emotionally focused oriented therapist understands that emotions do not inhibit the therapeutic process, but rather it is clients' inability to manage and use their emotions well that is the problem. Emotions are connected to our most essential needs, including attachment, and prepare and guide us in important situations to take action towards meeting our needs.[73]

Clients undergoing EFT learn to better identify, experience, explore, make sense of, transform, and flexibly manage their emotional experiences. EFT's main goals are to enlarge and restructure important emotional responses, instigate and nurture a secure bond between individuals, and help to shift each person's perspective of an experience while initiating new ways of interacting that are favorable for relationships.[74]

The experiential approach utilized by EFT-oriented therapists consists of their concentrating on and reflecting clients' emotions, validating and accepting clients' experiences, attuning to and empathically exploring clients' situations, expanding clients' experiences with questions,

---

[72] Group Therapy.org (2013); Johnson (2004, 2005); Tartakovsky (2011).

[73] Johnson (2004, 2005); Tartakovsky (2011).

[74] Good Therapy.org (2013); Johnson (2004, 2005).

and finally, guiding clients to participate in activities that foster a different processing of their experiences.[75]

It is well known that dogs react immediately to the presence of an emotion. Therefore, when a therapy dog is in the presence of a client who is experiencing an emotion, the dog will immediately react to this behavior in a validating and empathic manner. I have seen my own therapy dogs react to a client by getting up from where they were lying, going to the client and nudging, pawing, or licking him or her, which, in my opinion, indicates that the dog is aware of the client's emotional experience. Other providers of AAP have also noted that in some cases the dogs can be aware of an emotion before the client and therapist become aware of it and that AAP and EFT appear to be a helpful milieu for a client's emotional work.[76]

For stories that portray an EFT orientation, see the vignettes of Brittany and Susan in Chapter 11, Peter in Chapter 12, those of Deborah, Melanie, and Tiffany in Chapter 13, and both family vignettes in Chapter 14.

---

[75] Johnson (2004).

[76] Chandler (2012); Eggiman (2006); Fine (2010); Jalongo (2005); Jalongo, Astorino, and Bomboy (2004); King (2007); Wilkes (2009); Zilcha-Mano, Mikulincer, and Shaver (2011).

Chapter
10

Therapeutic Roles for the
Animal Co-Therapist

Once you have determined that a person is suitable for AAP, how does the therapy dog help facilitate the therapy process? The therapy dog acts as co-therapist in a variety of ways. First, a therapist often appears less threatening when a friendly therapy dog is present. Thus, the therapy dog helps to put clients at ease, to be cooperative, and to trust the therapist more easily. For example, Sacks reports the following about a therapy dog named Sara: When Sara entered Sean's treatment her involvement with him made him enjoy and look forward to the sessions. It also removed some of the pressure of relating just to me. For patients who are constricted, feel exposed and do not find talking about themselves a pleasant experience, use of the animal in therapy positively defuses this.[1]

The therapy dog also acts as an icebreaker and helps to establish the relationship between the client and

---

[1] Sacks (2008, p. 51).

therapist.[2] The therapy dog can be a subject for launching a conversation and can act as a catalyst for discussion or disclosure. For example, a young girl tried to touch a bird in a therapist's office. The bird hissed, and the therapist indicated, "must ask permission." The girl replied, "I know what you mean." The therapist showed the young girl how to touch the bird, stating the "bird doesn't like to be touched in certain places." The young girl repeated, "I know what you mean." The girl eventually disclosed that she had been sexually abused by one of her grandparents.[3] In these ways, the therapy dog can help people feel less self-conscious and more comfortable around the therapist, which helps to build the relationship between client and therapist.

Therapy dogs provide unconditional positive regard, love, and encourage mutual acceptance of the client.[4] Even when dogs are scolded, they still try to please and show how they love you by obeying or wagging their tails. This behavior also parallels how children try to please adults, even after the adult has hurt the child physically or psychologically. This tendency to please in a human may

[2] Berry et al. (2012); Chandler (2005, 2012); Eggiman (2006); Fine (2010); Jalongo, Astorino, and Bomboy (2004); King (2007); Lefkowitz et al. (2005); Minatrea and Wesley (2008); Parshall (2003); Peters (2011); Parish-Plass (2008); Sacks (2008); Shubert (2012b); Walsh (2009); Wilkes (2009); Zilcha-Mano, Mikulincer, and Shaver (2011).

[3] Fine (2010, p. 176).

[4] Chandler (2005, 2012); Eggiman (2006); Fine (2010); Foreman and Crosson (2012); Friesen (2010); Golin and Walsh (1994); Lange et al. (2006); Miller (2010);Parish-Plass (2008); Pitts (2005); Reichert (1998); Sacks (2008); Skloot (2009); Walsh (2009); Wilkes (2009); Zamir (2006); Zilcha-Mano, Mikulincer, and Shaver (2011).

become pathological and would then need to be worked through.

Moreover, clients can satisfy a need for love and affection when they touch/pet/cuddle the animal. In mothering the therapy dog, one is also mothering the self.[5]

The therapist and therapy dog can also act as role models.[6] This dynamic objectively displays a parent-child interaction. In a similar vein, therapy dogs can demonstrate appropriate, healthy boundaries.[7] For example, my therapy dog Loki will emit a small noise when people grab his feet. If you ask for his paw, he will give it, but when his paw is grabbed, he vocalizes inappropriate touch for him. Here, Loki role models, especially for children, that it is okay to say no to someone touching them.

In addition, clients and especially children might regulate their behavior when animals are present.[8] See Chapter 14, which discusses dogs in group therapy, for an example of this process.

Clients might also project their feelings onto the dog, which can allow the therapist to bring those feelings into the clients' awareness. For example, an angry client fantasizes that the dog will attack him/her, which can be a projection of his/her own rage onto the dog. In processing the feelings of anger in relation to the dog, the client

---

[5] Chandler (2005, 2012); Fine (2010); Hanselman (2001); Lange et al. (2006); Miller (2010); Parish-Plass (2008); Pitts (2005); Sacks (2008); Wilkes (2009); Zilcha-Mano, Mikulincer, and Shaver (2011).

[6] Delta Society (2000); Fine (2010); Minatrea and Wesley (2008); Parish-Plass (2008); Walsh (2009); Zilcha-Mano, Mikulincer, and Shaver (2011).

[7] Wilkes (2009).

[8] Berry et al. (2012); Chandler (2005, 2012); Fine (2010); Geist (2011); Lefkowitz et al. (2005); Minatrea and Pitts (2005); Wesley (2008).

becomes aware of his/her own feelings of anger. With children., we can access this projection by asking what the dog might be dreaming, thinking, or feeling, and this process allows the safe projection of a child's inner process onto the therapy dog.[9]

Figure 10.1 Hobbes, Lynn & Loki

The therapy dog can act as an intermediary. The client or the therapist can initiate this process. For example, a client might indicate that the dog looks sad, and when probed by the therapist about why the dog is sad, the client might indicate some of his or her own concerns or worries. Alternatively, with children., the therapist can ask questions on behalf of the therapy dog or can pretend that the dog whispers questions to the therapist and then state them as if the dog were asking them. This might help the child feel less threatened and more responsive to the questions.[10] Walsh reports another possible scenario from the work of

---

[9] Chandler (2005, 2012); Fine (2010); Lange et al. (2006); Parish-Plass (2008); Pitts (2005); Reichert (1998); Shubert (2012b); Walsh (2009); Zamir (2006).

[10] Chandler (2005, 2012); Fine (2010); Parish-Plass (2008); Reichert (1998); Shubert (2012b); Walsh (2009).

David Wohlsifer, a family therapist working with his therapy dog Jake:

> When Sean began to tell his story of childhood sexual abuse he started to sob. My therapy dog, Jake, came over and nuzzled his snout into his face. Sean hugged Jake tightly and continued to tell his story while I sat watching my co-therapist Jake do his work. After Sean finished his story, I praised him for his strength and courage in going to such a personal and painful place in sharing his story with me. Sean looked up and said, "I didn't tell my story to you; I told it to Jake."[11]

If a client demonstrates anger or wants to harm the dog, the therapist could ask, "what is it that the dog is doing that promotes that thought/feeling/behavior"? Then, the therapist can refer the response back to the client's problems/behaviors/thoughts. Perhaps it is something that the client doesn't like about him or herself; in this way, an unrecognized anger is brought to light. Likewise, negative reactions to therapy dogs, especially fear reactions, can lead to the processing of fears. See the story of Deborah on "being seen and not heard" in Chapter 13.

The therapy dog's behavior can also be utilized to jump-start a discussion of other human behaviors, such as physical pain, sex, cleanliness, relationships, and so forth.[12]

---

[11] Walsh (2009, p. 495).

[12] Chandler (2005, 2012); Fine (2010); Sacks (2008).

For example, when Meika, my retriever mix co-therapist, started moving more slowly as she aged, some clients asked what was wrong. When I informed them that she had arthritis, this knowledge often allowed them to process some of their physical pain or limitations, which also allows them to access their thoughts and feelings related to the changes in their physical capacities.

As the majority of communication with animals can be visual and/or non-verbal, which is typically genuine and difficult to fake or hide, we can determine valuable information merely by watching the client and therapy dog interact. Some researchers have indicated that this information can be diagnostically helpful and therefore therapeutically helpful.[13]

Moreover, according to several authors, AAP can influence attachment in many different ways.[14] Some of these have been mentioned above, such as fostering trust, safety, communication, and other positive connections between the human-animal bond. Attachment is possibly one of the most important human processes, as it begins in infancy and continues through the life span.

Geist and Walsh also indicate that when the therapy dog fosters laughter in a client, this also influences how the client forms attachment.[15] Geist describes an example in which a therapy dog attempts to give a toy to a client who is upset, which promotes laughter.[16] Because of this positive

---

[13] Butler (2004); Chandler (2005); Fine (2010); Prothmann et al. (2005); Reichert (1998).

[14] Geist (2011); Grado (2011); Hanselman (2001); Parish-Plass (2008); Shubert (2012a); Wilkes (2009).

[15] Geist (2011); Walsh (2009).

[16] Geist (2011).

reaction from the client, the dog continues to attempt to interact with the client, again fostering laughter. I have seen this many times in my own private practice when clients become distressed, and my therapy dog reacts by going to the clients, nudging them with his/her nose, pawing them, and then attempting to lick them. The client usually smiles or laughs, which encourages the therapy dog to continue the behavior. Geist indicates that this behavior is similar to when a child interacts with parents or caregivers and is positively reinforced by them, which then promotes attachment and social bonding between the two.[17] Geist also states that this attachment between the dog and the client can then be transferred to the therapist.[18]

Similarly, when a therapy dog reacts to a client's emotional distress by attempting to comfort the client by licking him or her, this behavior can result in the client shifting from pain to laughter. Chandler indicates that a therapy dog can temporarily shift clients away from some disabling pain they are experiencing when processing their difficulties and experiences.[19] She further indicates that this experience might encourage clients to work harder and longer in therapy and therefore benefit from it. I have seen this process at work: When a therapy dog reacts to clients' pain, either they will attempt to comfort themselves by petting the therapy dog, or the therapy dog will go to them and lick or lie beside them. This process can sometimes result in clients shifting from sadness to laughter.

Chandler notes that therapy animals can facilitate conditions that promote faster recovery when the therapy

---

[17] Geist (2011).
[18] Ibid.
[19] Chandler (2005, 2012).

animal provides temporary support, helps clients to develop deeper trust more quickly in the therapist when they see how the therapy animal relates to the therapist, and facilitates the therapist's empathy for clients when the therapist reflects the therapy animal's interaction with them.[20] Chandler also notes that a therapy animal augments the therapeutic relationship or the continuation of the therapist-client relationship by helping to build rapport, trust, and empathy.[21] Many of the vignettes presented in subsequent chapters also demonstrate this augmentation of the therapeutic relationship.

Walsh notes that when patients report that they or someone in their family is abusing or threatening to abuse the family pet, this behavior can indicate domestic violence in the family home, which is something that can then be processed in the patient's therapy.[22] The presence of a therapy animal might prompt disclosure of such abuse or threat to a family pet.

Parish-Plass and Walsh also note that reenactments of relationships can be played out with a family pet, as I have seen with my therapy dogs.[23] The following excerpt from Walsh exemplifies this type of interaction:

> Sondra consulted with me about a troubling dilemma; she felt controlled and imprisoned in her apartment by her small dog, Rex. She was becoming increasingly isolated and depressed. She couldn't leave Rex alone; she

---

[20] Chandler (2005).

[21] Ibid.

[22] Walsh (2009).

[23] Parish-Plass (2008); Walsh (2009).

thought he looked depressed [her projection] much of the time and would be too upset. I asked her more about this bond. She replied, "I'm confused; he's very cute and I'm sort of attached to him but not sure I love him. Yet I feel that he needs me and I can't abandon him. He whimpers if I don't want him in my bed. So I let him sleep with me, but I toss and turn all night. It's terrible; I don't know what to do." Asked how she acquired the pup, she said that she had been in a serious relationship with Sylvio, very much wanting to marry and have a child together. However, his possessive, controlling behavior led her to break up with him, despite his pleas not to leave him. At their last meeting to say goodbye, he surprised her with the gift of this puppy. She had not wanted a dog, but felt obliged to accept it, as she felt guilty leaving Sylvio when he loved her so much. "Hah! She interjected, I left the man but I can't leave the dog he gave me!

Sondra brought Rex to our next session for me to meet him. She immediately held up the puppy, saying "look at him, doesn't he look depressed? I think he knows I'm confused about him." Sondra sat down, cradled Rex in her arms, and smiled lovingly at him through tears. I suggested that maybe her tangled emotions about Rex could help us understand some unresolved issues in her relationship with Sylvio. In our discussion, she acknowledged that she had trouble standing up for herself not only with Rex, but with men, and feared being controlled like her mother was by her father. As she gained ability in setting limits with Rex and resumed going out with friends, her depression lifted and she felt more loving toward the pup and toward Sylvio. With new confidence in asserting her needs, she requested couples therapy with Sylvio to see if the relationship could succeed on new terms, and if not, to say goodbye for good. But, she added, either way, she now was sure about keeping Rex in her life and her heart.[24]

Sacks indicates that an unplanned intervention can result in awareness of the client's own behaviors, as illustrated below:

> Sara being the pushy, dominant dog that she was often went over to Joan looking for attention. The patient would be petting her while talking to me. At the same time she was telling her to go and sit down. She was unaware of the mixed message she was sending to the dog. I pointed out how she was petting Sara at the same time as making a request for her to go away. Joan became

---

[24] Walsh (2009, p. 496).

aware of this, stopped petting, and tried to tell her to lie down. Sara 'forced' her to tell her firmly before she listened.[25]

Figure 10.2 Loki & Lynn at a Health Fair

Parish-Plass, Miller, and Sacks posit that therapy dogs can provide "corrective object relationship" experiences.[26] They differentiate this term from our usual term of a corrective emotional experience, as therapy dogs provide tactile fulfillment, are responsive in similar ways to humans, and can be playful, engaged, warm, and comforting, which can elicit spontaneous relational reactions from clients who might have been deprived of this type of interaction.

Parish-Plass indicates that AAP encourages an environment of friendliness and normalcy in a therapy setting, promotes a sense of control, improves self-esteem

---

[25] Sacks (2008, p. 515).

[26] Parish-Plass (2008); Miller (2010); Sacks (2008).

and the adaptation or internalization of healthier representations or coping mechanisms, and can promote empathy even in people with attachment issues.[27]

Finally, when a therapy dog retires or dies, this event can be used to work through grief and reactions to separation, abandonment, or death.[28] For example, Sacks describes a client's reaction to her therapy dog:

> Over time Jack noticed Sara slowing down and it brought out associations to how he handled or didn't handle very well the loss of his other cats. He just dropped them off for euthanasia and did not want to be around. He mourned that response. Thus, Sara was both a source for associations and memories and, in particular, experiences related to grief and loss, and regret in this case. She enabled him to have more of his feelings.[29]

---

[27] Parish-Plass (2008).

[28] Chandler (2005, 2012); Delta Society (2005); Fine (2010); Levinson (1997); Parish-Plass (2008); Pitts (2005); Zilcha-Mano, Mikulincer, and Shaver (2011).

[29] Sacks (2008, p. 510).

Chapter
11

Animal-Assisted
Psychotherapy Interventions
with Children

Animal-assisted psychotherapy (AAP) with children can be very powerful. Children automatically feel accepted and loved by animals in their lives. Children also feel less threatened when a friendly dog is with a stranger, and they will also see the therapy dog as a transitional object in connecting with an adult figure.[1]

The following case vignettes illustrate planned and unplanned interventions. The planned interventions relate to children who have a pervasive developmental disorder, learning to accept and give touch, all children learning how to use nonverbal social cues, using the therapy dogs' reactions to human emotions to process feelings about past experiences, helping a child become a child again, building self-esteem and confidence, and learning self-control, to

---

[1] Chandler (2005, 2012); Fine (2010); Geist (2011); Hanselman (2001); Levinson (1997); Parish-Plass (2008); Reichert (1998); Wilkes (2009).

self soothe, and to understand how one's behavior impacts others.

The unplanned interventions demonstrate the therapy dog's unconditional acceptance, the therapist and therapy dog's compassion and empathy, creating safety to process past sexual abuse, and learning to show compassion to others.

Mark and Meika – the Receiver and Giver of Hugs

Mark was an only child. Both parents had significant physical and mental health issues. When I first met Mark, he was 10 years old but appeared younger both physically and developmentally. He clearly demonstrated characteristics of a pervasive developmental disorder, such as difficulty tolerating being touched, held, or hugged by others, impoverished eye contact and facial expressions, friends who were typically younger than he, difficulty sustaining conversations, preservative communication, and difficulty transitioning from one task to another. Upon meeting Mark and his parents, I knew some of the struggles that he and his family faced and knew that AAP would be beneficial for Mark and, indirectly, his family. We all agreed that my primary work would be with Mark, as both of his parents needed Mark to learn social skills that they were unable to help him learn, as well as how to explore his unfamiliar emotions in a safe and healthy way.

Using AAP, I knew that we could help Mark learn aspects of non-verbal communication, specifically the use and importance of eye contact, facial expressions, and tone of voice. Meika's temperament was a perfect fit for the work that Mark needed to accomplish. Because Meika is a dog that is sometimes unresponsive to treats, much of her training was accomplished by using eye contact, hand gestures, facial expressions, and tone of voice, all of which could help facilitate Mark's learning of these skills.

Figure 11.1 Meika Sleeping

So, Mark, Meika, and I began to help Mark learn important social skills. Each session involved having Mark engage with Meika and getting her to perform a trick for him, such as come, sit, stay, paw, roll over, and so forth. Part of this work involved helping Mark use the tone of his voice to encourage cooperation from Meika and, when she was uncooperative, to change his tone to encourage her cooperation. Mark quickly learned to use a "happy" tone of voice to have Meika come to him and give him her paw and, when Meika was uncooperative, to use a "stern" tone, but not shouting or loud volume, to engage her with him.

Another important aspect of this work was the use of eye-to-eye contact and facial expressions. To gain Meika's focused attention, Mark was encouraged to use eye-to-eye contact and a smiling face so that Meika would understand that "good things" are about to happen. When eye contact is not made with Meika or most dogs, we do not have their full attention, and they will be unlikely to perform the requested task. The same can be said of people. Nonetheless, it is important to use the appropriate amount of eye contact; if we stare intently with a serious face, the dog might see us as threatening. So, Mark was encouraged to look at Meika and smile. Initially, he was only able to do this very briefly but eventually was able to maintain eye contact for many seconds, which facilitated his gaining her attention. Having a child such as Mark learn eye contact with a well-trained dog allows him to develop mastery and comfort with the behavior until he is then able to use this behavior with people, which can be initially intimidating. When we use a happy or pleasant tone of voice, we understand that good things are happening or that the person is pleased to see us and wants to interact positively with us.

One day a few months after beginning his therapy work, Mark came to his session and appeared upset and agitated. Upon entering the therapy room, Mark ran to the couch, jumped on it, and placed his body in a fetal position with his face buried in the couch cushions. His voice was shaky and weak; he was difficult to hear, and it was hard to understand what he was saying. I sat on the floor beside where he lay on the couch, which signaled to Meika to sit beside me. She came over, sniffed at Mark, and tried to give him a kiss, but he pulled his hand away. During the next 15 minutes, Mark tearfully explored how some friends at school had been mean to him; during this time, Meika attempted to nudge Mark with her nose to comfort him, but he continued to ignore her. I reflected his distress and validated his feelings. With both of us demonstrating to Mark that he was valued and cared for, he began to slowly relax his body and eventually turned his face towards us, which gave Meika just the opportunity she needed to give Mark a kiss on his face. This action was the shift that Mark needed to know that he was loved and cared for. He sat up, encouraged Meika to join him on the couch, and she eagerly complied. Within a few minutes, Mark was laughing and playing with Meika, his early distress dissipated.

Mark's work continued in this vein, and during that time Mark's confidence and self-esteem grew as he mastered Meika and himself. Part of this work included encouraging and allowing Mark to hug Meika and for Meika to give him a "hug." To ameliorate any concern for this activity, I first modeled the giving of the hug. I demonstrate this behavior by kneeling in front of the dog, leaning in, and embracing the dog with both hands. If the child is uncomfortable with this action, then we break the behavior into smaller parts, such as touching the dog, sitting beside the dog and petting it, or giving the dog a sideways hug with one hand. Until the child expresses comfort with each of these behaviors, the full frontal hug is not requested. Later, once giving a hug has been safely and comfortable mastered, I model receiving a "hug" from Meika.

Figure 11.2 Hobbes Giving a "Hug"

Receiving a hug requires the furry facilitator's paws to be placed on the person's shoulders, but before this can happen, the child must first hold the dog's paws, feel the claws, sit very close to the dog, and allow the dog to rest his or her body and/or paws on the child in a lying position and then in a seated position so the child becomes accustomed to the dog's weight gently resting on him or her. The "hug" activity requires the child to kneel before the dog in close proximity so that the child's knees are almost touching the dog's paws. The child's bottom rests on his or her heels, and the furry facilitator sits directly in front of the child. When the child is ready, s/he pats the shoulders with hands and says "hug." The furry facilitator will then sit back and raise the front paws. The child is then required to lean in a little as the furry facilitator rests the paws on the child's shoulder, thus giving the child a hug.

This activity with Mark and Meika took place over several weeks.

When Mark mastered his discomfort with this touch and began to feel more at ease, he asked me if he could show his mother. Mark then gleefully demonstrated the hug to his mother, who applauded and praised him. Mark then ran to his mother, threw his arms around her neck, and hugged her. Mark's mother, with her head over Mark's shoulder, looked at me. I could see tears in her eyes as she welcomed the hug from Mark. Mark then let go of his mother, ran back to Meika, and gave her a hug, too. Mark was so pleased with himself that he could hardly contain his excitement. In the next few weeks, Mark continued to practice the hug with Meika, both giving and receiving, and this process eventually transferred to his being comfortable giving and receiving hugs from humans.

Brittany: Processing Recent Incest and the Power of a Loving Dog, Loki

Brittany, an 11-year-old girl, was the only child of divorced parents. The parents divorced when the mother discovered that Brittany was being sexually abused by her father. Her mother had, at Brittany's request, found a therapist to help Brittany explore her feelings and thoughts concerning her abuse, reporting her abuse to the police, her father's later imprisonment for the incest, and her parents' divorce. After several months of working with the therapist, Brittany was not opening up to the therapist, and little therapeutic work was being accomplished. Brittany asked her mother to stop going to therapy, and her mother agreed. A year or more later, Brittany started acting out angrily in school and at home. Her mother was at a loss as to what was happening and suggested that they try to find a therapist again to help Brittany. Brittany agreed and they found us.

Given that Brittany was a dog lover and her mother was unable to have a dog where they lived, her mother thought that we would be a good fit for helping Brittany. So, we met to discuss what was going on for Brittany. Although many state laws require that therapists allow parents access to a child's therapy records, in some cases I ask parents to waive that right. If the parents agree, they sign a form in front of their children so that the children understand that their therapy is confidential. Brittany's mother agreed to waive her rights to her medical records. Nonetheless, I always stipulate to children that if they are engaging in dangerous behaviors, we will need to tell the parents. I believe that allowing children this kind of freedom in therapy is important, especially in cases of incest.

So, Brittany, Loki, and I met weekly. Initially, Brittany was hesitant to talk about her past sexual abuse, her father's arrest and imprisonment, or her parent's divorce. She was able to talk about feeling angry and confused. During these times, she would sit on the couch, with Loki often sitting beside her. She would pet him as she talked about her anger and confusion. After several weeks, during one session Brittany became notably angry and was raising her voice. I knew that Loki would not like this and would jump off the couch and come to me, which is what he did. Brittany noticed this behavior and asked what was wrong. I told her that Loki has never liked people raising their voices, often becomes scared when this happens, and will seek comfort and reassurance from me that he will not be hurt. This was the catalyst I had been hoping and waiting for. Brittany's flood gates opened, and she cried as she tried to console Loki and encourage him back to the couch with her. She cooed with Loki and told him that she knew what it was like to be scared of someone and not have anyone to turn to. I queried what she meant by this, and she began to relate how her father had started molesting her at age 6 and how scared and confused she was. She also related how he threatened that no one would believe her and that if she told, he would hurt her and her mother. It was this latter threat that kept Brittany silent for three years, the fear of him hurting her mother.

In subsequent sessions, Brittany would often lie on the couch with Loki lying in front of her, almost like a body pillow. Over the following months, Brittany explored more of her abuse while lying with Loki, who would often turn to her when she began to cry and would attempt to soothe her by licking her arms or face, whichever he could reach most easily. She later told me that it was Loki's loving acceptance of her while she related the horror of those three long years that helped her to feel connected to me and that his actions allowed her to feel "unconditional acceptance" from us while she was unable to accept herself or what had happened to her.

Figure 11.3 Loki Providing Comfort

During several months of therapy, Brittany spent most of it cuddling and petting Loki and soothing herself as she spoke about her abuse, and as she soothed herself in therapy, her "acting out" behaviors outside of therapy ceased. In many sessions, she would lie on the couch with Loki acting as her pillow while she cried and told of her abuse. At times, she was unable to continue talking about her abuse and would gently hug Loki until she could continue processing her sadness, anger, and confusion as well as self-blame for the abuse.

Through Loki's open acceptance of Brittany, she was able to process all of the issues she had initially presented with and was even able to work through the blame she experienced concerning her father's imprisonment and her parents' divorce. Toward the end of our meetings, Brittany asked that her mother join the session from time to time. During these sessions she discovered how strong she had become as she sat with Loki and shared some of what happened to her with her mother. And when her mother cried, she let Loki go and encouraged him to console her mother, just as he had done for her.

David: ADHD - Learning Impulse Control

David, an 11-year-old male, came to see me when his divorced parents were struggling with how to help him control his impulsivity. David had been evaluated by his pediatrician and had been diagnosed with attention deficit hyperactivity disorder, combined type. David, his parents, and I all agreed that appropriate treatment for him would consist of helping him learn how to regulate his emotions, how to relax, and then to establish impulse control.

One of the first interventions I planned for David was for him to engage with Meika in her favorite game, "bubbles." In this game the child is required to blow bubbles for Meika so that she can jump and catch them. Initially, David, like most children, blew lots of small bubbles. After a few minutes of chasing and jumping to catch the small bubbles, Meika got tired. I explained that she likes to chase and catch big bubbles.

So, to help Meika, David was encouraged to blow big bubbles for her. We then practiced taking a deep breath in and blowing out slowly, thus producing larger bubbles. Once David mastered the process of breathing slowly, allowing him to blow larger bubbles for Meika, she became quickly reengaged with the game. David had also just learned how to perform diaphragmatic breathing, which is a relaxation technique. Later, when David became agitated in the session, he was encouraged to pretend to blow large bubbles for Meika. After a short time, this pretend activity helped David to calm himself and engage more appropriately in the session. David was also encouraged to use this technique whenever he found himself becoming agitated or impulsive. So that David could practice the game, I presented him with a small bottle of bubbles. David was delighted with this gift and promised to practice blowing larger bubbles for Meika.

Figure 11.4 Hobbes Playing Bubbles

In a later session, Loki was present to work with David. David had been working hard on using the bubble-breathing technique and other strategies to regulate his emotions. In this session David had been discussing some troubling experiences at school. While exploring these experiences, he was petting Loki. During this petting,

David's hand drifted down towards Loki's paws. David then attempted to hold Loki's paw. At this time Loki emitted a low noise and quickly removed his paw from David's hand. David asked what had just happened. I explained to David that my guess was that some time ago, someone had grabbed Loki's paw and hurt it. Hence, Loki now exhibited a boundary when people tried to touch or grab his paws. Nonetheless, Loki is always more than willing to offer his paw to be held when asked for it, but he does not like it when his paw is grabbed or held without his permission. David expressed some sadness related to Loki being hurt and was able to liken this to his own experiences. I explained that, as Loki was unable to speak, his only method of communication was to make a noise and remove his paw. This process allowed us to explore healthy ways to express boundaries when others violate them. We explored that, sometimes when David's brother tries to take his Game Boy toy away, David often reacts angrily by pushing and yelling. David was then able to use his diaphragmatic breathing behavior to allow time for him to become calm and consider a more appropriate behavior for himself in similar situations. David expressed that when his brother next attempted to take his Game Boy toy from him, he would take a deep breath and state his feelings about what his brother was doing and what he wanted his brother to do. We role-played this in different scenarios.

Several months later, David proudly stated that he had helped his brother to calm himself when he had a "meltdown." David further explained that he had shown his brother, just as I had done before, how to blow large bubbles so that he could use this technique when he became distressed. I validated David's ability to help his brother in this manner. David's therapy work on emotional regulation, stress reduction, relaxation, and impulse control continued for several months. During this time David would often ask questions regarding Meika and Loki. One of the questions he asked was how they got along and if they ever got into fights. I indicated that generally the two dogs got along well, but occasionally they would get into arguments or fights. I also indicated that they had never hurt each other, but sometimes they intimidated each other. I explained that this is typical behavior for dogs. This information allowed David to explore some of the arguments and fights he and his brother had recently been experiencing. At this time I chose to use my own experiences with my dogs to parallel David's situations. I explained that when Meika and Loki growled and started to fight, this upset me, as I feared that one of them might get hurt. I also explained that I saw it as part of my parent role to stop them from hurting each other and to try to help them work things out. David expressed that this situation helped him understand how his parents might be feeling when he and his brother physically fought. He was then asked to explore how he sometimes perceived his parents' taking his younger brother's side more often. This allowed us to explore the social mores according to which older children are supposed to set an example for younger children, and adults often expect an older child to act in a more adult manner to help the younger child learn appropriate behaviors. I explained that his parents were likely not preferring or taking his brother's side but that they expected him to act as an appropriate role model to help his brother grow up to be like him and his parents.

Figure 11.5 Loki Teaching Impulse Control

As David was using the relaxation and emotional regulation strategies, we continued to work on impulse control. For this objective, I use a trick with Loki in which he is required to balance a treat on his nose, wait until he hears the command to have the treat, and then try to catch the treat in his mouth. David was well aware of Loki's love for food and especially treats, so he was able to understand how difficult it was for Loki to manage his impulse to take the treat before the release word was given. Again, this behavior parallels how difficult it was for David to control his own impulses. To make this parallel, I used the consequences for Loki: when he is able to control his impulses, he obtains the treat he desires, whereas when he is unable to control his impulses, he does not obtain the treat. This activity allowed us to explore many of David's impulse-control issues and to use the parallel of the nose/treat trick to help David stop, think, and choose a behavior that leads to his desired outcome. When David would come back to the sessions and reported that, from time to time, he had failed to maintain his impulse control, we explored the obstacles that got in the way and figured out ways for him to improve his impulse control.

Figure 11.6 Loki Demonstrating Impulse Control

Crystal: Building Self Esteem

Crystal, a 10-year-old female, was brought to therapy by her parents. They indicated that she was a very anxious, shy child, with no friends, and was always very hesitant to try anything new. The family had recently given their own dog up for adoption, as they were unable to provide for the dog. I learned from Crystal that she blamed herself for the dog's being given up for adoption as she was unable to manage taking the dog on walks, and so it often toileted inside the home, which the parents refused to tolerate.

At our first meeting, Crystal appeared to be a shy, reticent child. After meeting with her several times, however, she opened into a bright, articulate child who had a lot of things to say and appeared mature beyond her years. It seemed that her family life had resulted in Crystal forgetting that she was a child and how to relate to children her own age. Part of her family dynamics was for her to take care of her much younger sister; she became parentified and very protective of her younger sister.

Part of Crystal's therapy was to help her learn to be a child again and relate in a child's ways. She reported that her school peers never seemed to like her, and she did not understand why. She was quite content to sit on my sofa and talk about her problems in a very adult-like manner, so much so that I often thought of this 10-year-old as a 40-year-old female; there was no child presence. It was obvious to me that in helping her learn to play with the therapy dogs, we could help her learn how to interact with other children. Dogs are good mirrors of children's behaviors because dogs are always in the moment, not worried about the past or the future, just what is happening now. Initially, Crystal was hesitant to play with Meika or Loki, whoever was present for her session. She reported that she really did not know how to play with them. She would willingly talk to them as if they were another person, but interacting with Meika or Loki in other ways was unknown to her.

As described above, one of Meika's favorite games is "bubbles." I chose this activity for Crystal, as Meika engages in it willingly, and many of the children I have worked with love to blow bubbles. Crystal, however, had never learned how to blow bubbles, so we started with learning how to blow bubbles. Of course, this frustrated Meika as she was always animated to play bubbles but wasn't getting any bubbles to chase and burst. Once Crystal mastered how to blow big bubbles, she and Meika played for some time, and Crystal started to laugh and learn how to play.

With Loki, Crystal learned how to play in other ways, such as throwing a ball and having Loki either retrieve it or catch it in his mouth and getting him to perform many of his tricks. During this process I helped Crystal to become aware of her non-verbal behaviors that encouraged Loki and Meika to play with her, such as her body posture and her facial expression. Crystal typically did not smile, and she reported feeling awkward when asked to smile. She was encouraged to practice smiling with the dogs, as this is a language they understand as welcoming and engaging, as do other children. Instead of holding her body in a closed-off manner, she was encouraged to relax her body and have a more open stance. She practiced this with Loki and Meika and noted how they reacted to her body language.

As time went on, Crystal became more assertive and would ask me to show her how to have the dogs perform the tricks they had learned. As she learned how to successfully approximate a behavior, she became more confident in her own abilities. We worked with Meika and Loki to role-play how she might engage with a peer at school and attempt to make a friend. As each week passed, her self-esteem and confidence developed. Instead of being the serious young woman I first met, she slowly became more age appropriate in her behaviors. Eventually, she reported playing with some girls at recess and sitting with them at lunch. Crystal started asking her mother for more age-appropriate clothing to help her fit in with her school peers.

Toward the end of our therapy, Crystal started asking more and more about training dogs and how to manage them, how to house train them, how to manage walking dogs as they got bigger and stronger. Of course, having Meika and Loki helped with this growth for Crystal. Later, the family decided to try again with another dog. This time Crystal's confidence in her ability to understand her new pet's behaviors as well as how to train the dog allowed the family to keep this pet.

Richard: Developing Self Mastery and Frustration Tolerance

Richard came to therapy at the age of 6. His divorced parents were at a loss about his angry behaviors, such as hitting and biting other children or throwing and breaking objects. Upon meeting with Richard and his parents, I was initially uncertain that we could work together. Richard was very angry and behaving angrily; this behavior concerned me for the sake of Meika and Loki. If Richard was unable to promise that he would not intentionally hurt the dogs, even when he was really mad, I knew I would not be able to work with him. I had previously discussed this point with the parents prior to meeting Richard, and we decided to give it a try.

So, Richard came to his first session with his mother. When I went to the waiting area, Richard was speaking loudly and hitting a book. I quietly explained to Richard that in my office was a special dog, called Meika, who was very gentle and shy. I explained that if Richard was loud and animated Meika, she might be a little scared of him and might not want to play with him. I asked Richard if he wanted to meet Meika and if he would be willing to walk slowly and quietly into my office and use a soft voice to say hello to Meika; Richard agreed. We all walked back to my office, and when we entered the room, Meika was lying in a corner. She immediately got up and walked over to Richard, wagging her tail. He looked tentatively at me, and I assured him he could gently pet her, which he did. He immediately smiled, sat on the floor, and petted Meika. She, after a few moments, lay down on the floor beside him. While his mother and I talked for a few moments, Richard made himself more comfortable on the floor and continued to pet Meika. After a short while, he started to ask me questions about Meika, such as what kind of dog she was and why she was special. This process continued for about 20 minutes, and all the time Richard sat and petted Meika. His mother quietly commented that this was the calmest she had seen Richard in months.

Richard, Meika, and I met weekly to help Richard learn to self soothe and to manage his anger. Richard's therapy consisted of him soothing himself by petting Meika. As Meika lay beside him on the floor, he was encouraged to put his hand on Meika's belly and to match his breathing to hers. Thus, he learned to self soothe by slowing his breathing and keeping his body still. Whenever Richard became agitated or frustrated in session, he was asked to help calm Meika, as she would often withdraw from him when he would move fast. So, he would have to immediately stop what he was doing, sit on the floor, call Meika to come to him, and then pet her while matching his breathing to hers.

Figure 11.7 Hobbes Performing "Stick 'em up"

Another part of Richard's therapy consisted of engaging Meika in her numerous tricks. I chose Meika to help Richard because she can be uncooperative when others try to make her perform tricks, although, like my other dogs, she has been trained to perform tricks. Meika will typically do the tricks for me, but she sometimes will not engage with others when they want her to do tricks. I knew that this would simulate real life for Richard if Meika became stubborn and refused to comply with a command given by him.

Usually, Meika cooperated and performed whatever trick Richard asked of her. On rare occasions, she refused to cooperate with Richard, which frustrated him. At these times, he began to raise his voice and to move his body in jerky movements, which caused Meika to withdraw from him. So, he had to learn how to moderate his voice and body to encourage Meika's cooperation. There were several sessions in which Richard became frustrated by Meika's lack of cooperation. I empathized with his feelings and asked him if this is how his parents sometimes felt when they were unable to get Richard to cooperate with them. We brainstormed together on how to encourage Meika's cooperation, as even when we tried treats to encourage her to perform a trick, she sometimes still refused. At these times, we wondered what might be occurring for Meika that might explain why she would not play or interact with us. This interaction allowed Richard to project his own process onto Meika, and we helped Meika work through the problems, thus giving Richard space to explore his own processes in a safe manner. At other times, Richard was encouraged to persevere with Meika and to encourage her to perform the trick he wanted. Sometimes he was successful in getting Meika to complete the trick; at other times he was successful in managing his frustration and learning to walk away when his frustration began to turn to anger. At these times, he engaged with me to play a game or draw something. After several months of learning to self-soothe, tolerate frustration, and master his anger, Richard graduated from his therapy.

Susan: Rejection and Adoption

Susan's story is rather sad. Susan's biological mother had given up her legal rights to Susan when she was 11 years old. Her mother had broken up with Susan's biological father several years before and had been living with a boyfriend. Susan had a younger brother, and both were abused physically and emotionally by their mother and her boyfriend. They were also both neglected by their biological parents. Although Susan's father had indicated that he would take Susan but not her brother, when Susan's parents separated, he failed to do so. Thus, she remained with her mother and the mother's live-in boyfriend. This boyfriend later went on to abuse Susan sexually. This situation prompted child protective services to become involved. Susan and her brother were removed from the biological mother's home. Fortunately, they were placed with her mother's sister, who wanted to adopt both children.

Susan was also unusual in that she was very open to talking about her feelings and about her life experiences. One of her first questions was about the therapy dogs. She asked me how I had obtained the dogs. I explained that I had adopted the dogs from a rescue shelter. I also explained that Meika had been found running in a neighborhood, and no one had come to claim her. I had adopted her when she was approximately 6 months old. I indicated that Loki's story was a little different; he and a sibling were given up for adoption, as the family who had the parent dogs did not want to keep the puppies. I indicated that we had adopted Loki when he was 10 weeks old. This discussion allowed Susan to open up about her own concerns over being adopted by her aunt as well as feeling angry and upset because she missed her own mother. Often during these processes, Susan sat on the floor with either Meika or Loki beside her and petted the dog. When Susan became tearful, she would often bury her face into the dog's fur. In turn, Meika or Loki would often turn to Susan and lick her. Susan asked why they licked her. I suggested that perhaps it was their way of trying to say she would be okay and that they understood the pain because they too had been adopted. I also suggested that perhaps they were trying to offer hope that being adopted would be okay for her, too.

Susan and I spent several sessions discussing her anger and distress regarding her removal from her mother's home. During these sessions, Susan would often sit or lie on the sofa with either Meika or Loki, petting them as she softly spoke about her feelings. During one such session, Susan was exploring her anger. As she became noticeably angry, her body tensed, and her voice became louder and tense. Loki, who had been lying asleep beside her, suddenly got up and jumped down off the couch. He immediately came over to me and sat down beside me, nudging my hand as if to say, "comfort me." Susan reported being shocked by Loki's action and sadly expressed that she had not meant to do anything wrong and did not mean to scare Loki away from her. I explained that Loki does not like it when people become angry, and so he was distancing himself from her anger and seeking comfort with me. I indicated to Susan that she had done nothing wrong and was not behaving badly in any way. This discussion led to Susan exploring several instances in which her mother and father had argued loudly, and she had sought refuge in her bedroom. As Susan became calm, Loki returned to her side. Susan said to Loki,

"I wish you had been with me to help me through that; it was horrible." I validated Susan's feelings and her actions to seek refuge and to help herself cope when her parents argued.

Later, in a session when Susan was talking about missing her mother, Loki was lying beside her on his side. While Susan was petting Loki, he started to lift one of his hind legs. It was then that Susan realized Loki was a boy dog. When she saw his penis, which was covered in fur, she immediately withdrew her hand and indicated what she had seen. She immediately began to cry, and Loki rolled over, sat up, and licked the tears streaming down her face. This interaction allowed Susan to start exploring the sexual abuse she had experienced by her mother's boyfriend. Throughout this process, as Susan wept, she told her story and often stopped when she found it difficult to continue. It was at this time that Loki often nudged her leg or hand as if to tell her she could go on, and he would be there with her. Usually, when the sessions came to an end, Susan spent the last few minutes hugging and playing with Meika or Loki. It was wonderful to see how such a young child could explore these horrible experiences and yet be able to quickly revert back to being a child to play with the therapy dog.

At a later point, Susan came to a session in an agitated state. She had just returned from a week's vacation with the aunt who wished to adopt her. As she entered the room, she immediately flung herself on the sofa and was quickly joined by Meika. She explained that she had learned about becoming adopted and that her birth certificate might need to be changed. She indicated that she did not want her name to be changed; she wanted to keep her parents' last name and did not want her birth certificate to be changed.

I suggested that we call her aunt into the session to discuss Susan's concerns with her; Susan refused. I suggested that perhaps she could work out what she was to say to her aunt by talking it over with Meika. Susan agreed and moved to the other end of the sofa from where Meika lay. Susan then looked at Meika and stated the thought she had expressed earlier. I provided a little coaching, and she appeared to falter in what she wanted to say. We practiced what she wanted to say several times. At the end of the session, Susan indicated that she felt prepared and ready to have this discussion with her aunt. I suggested that we have her aunt come into the session so that Susan could tell her that she needed some one-on-one time to talk to her later, which she did. The following week Susan returned and happily reported that they had agreed to go ahead with the adoption with the proviso that Susan keep her given family name. Several months later, after Susan had resolved her abuse and her anger was no longer an issue, we terminated therapy.

Summary

In summary, one can see from these case vignettes how the therapy dog acts in an unintentional way as a transitional object, provides unconditional acceptance, helps to demonstrate how feelings can impact others, shows compassion, helps clients learn how to be assertive, provides safety, helps clients to feel cared for in order to explore difficult experiences, and through the dog's reactions to the human, helps clients learn how they impact others.

Additionally, in the planned interventions, we can see from Mark's vignette how the therapy dog helps clients learn to accept and give touch and to practice the use of nonverbal communication skills. With Crystal, we can see how the co-therapist helped her learn how to relate to other children and learn how to be a child again. AAP helped Richard to develop frustration tolerance and to better manage his anger. David's vignette demonstrates how AAP helped him learn to calm himself and practice self-soothing skills.

Many of the vignettes described above have utilized the orientations of play therapy, cognitive behavioral therapy, person-centered therapy, and an interpersonal process.

The vignettes of both Mark and Susan reflect an attachment orientation focus. In Mark's vignette, the attachment orientation occurs when Meika creates a safe "holding" environment, comfort, and acts as a "good-enough mother" to Mark. Similarly, in Susan's vignette, Loki creates the safe "holding" environment, provides unconditional acceptance and comfort, and acts as a "good-enough mother" to Susan.

The object relations (OR) orientation exists in the vignettes for David and Brittany. In David's vignette, we see the OR orientation when I explore the role of a "good-enough mother" in relation to my co-therapists and parallel that with the roles of David's parents. In the vignette for Brittany, the co-therapist Loki demonstrates the OR orientation as he "holds" Brittany's difficult emotions when he lies beside her and she pets him. Loki also fosters the creation of the transitional safe space when he acts as a transitional object for her, and he acts as a "good-enough mother" when he comforts her and is with her as she processes her abuse.

The vignettes of Susan, David, Richard, and Crystal demonstrate a behavioral therapy (BT) and/or an SFBT orientation. These vignettes use the game of "bubbles" to teach a self-soothing and calming behavior to the children. In Crystal's vignette, we also see an SFBT or BT process when I help her become aware of her non-verbal behaviors and how they impact her interaction with the co-therapists. Similarly, in Richard's vignette, we see a BT or SFBT process when Richard is encouraged to self-soothe by petting Meika or lying with her and matching his breathing to hers.

In Brittany's and Susan's vignettes, we see the use of an emotionally focused (EFT) orientation. The EFT orientation occurs in Brittany's vignette when I encourage her to focus on and process her emotions related to her abuse. This process is assisted by the presence of Loki, who helps to soothe and hold those emotions for her. Susan's vignette demonstrates EFT when she reacts to Loki moving away from her, which allows her to process feelings related to times when her parents argued and how this upset her. EFT also occurred when Susan was encouraged to explore her feelings regarding her sexual abuse and when Loki attempted to comfort her and stay with her, as if to hold her emotions.

Part of Richard's vignette demonstrates a cognitive orientation (CO) to his issues. The CO was demonstrated when Richard was unable to gain Meika's cooperation in performing tricks. Here, Richard was encouraged to "brainstorm" a response to why Meika was refusing to cooperate.

Finally, in David's vignette, we can see a psychodynamic orientation. The psychodynamic process occurs when David explores whether my co-therapists fight and asks other questions about them. When he asks these questions, he appears to be attempting to understand, through the discussion concerning the therapy dogs, some of his own issues related to his sibling and parents.

Many other examples of the orientations discussed in this book appear in the vignettes described above and in the following chapters. I have not illuminated all of these examples in the summaries at the end of these chapters. The illustrations provided are intended to show how AAP can be utilized with many different orientations. Other orientations that work with AAP include Gestalt, personal constructivist, humanistic, existential, and other orientations. These have not been illustrated, as they have not been explained earlier in the book. I am sure that many readers will have already identified various other orientations that have been or could be utilized within the framework of AAP.

Chapter

12

Animal-Assisted Psychotherapy Interventions with Adolescents

Adolescents can sometimes be the most challenging and most rewarding clients to work with. It has been my and other professionals' experience that to work with adolescents, one needs to have the patience of a saint and the forthrightness of Dr. Phil.

The following case vignettes involving adolescents clearly show the need to be forthright and patient when working with adolescents. Specifically, the case vignettes show planned interventions aimed at managing anger, developing social skills, learning to self soothe, paralleling a dog's experience with the clients' experience to aid in achieving goals regarding medication and grooming, and learning how to identify and use nonverbal behaviors.

The following case vignettes also demonstrate unplanned interventions, such as using clients' curiosity regarding the dog to understand their own defenses or the purpose of their attention-seeking behaviors, providing safety and comfort or the disclosure of difficult materials, how the therapy dog aids in establishing the therapeutic alliance, how the therapy dog inadvertently encourages the disclosure of self-harming behaviors, and how clients achieve comfort from the therapy dog.

Figure 12.1 Meika at 6 Months Old

Mandy: Coping with Depression/Bipolar Disorder

Mandy, a 13-year-old girl, came to me after she had been released from a nearby hospital for suicidal behaviors. Her mother reported that for the past year, Mandy had been cutting, was aggressive, and extremely moody. Although her mother was well groomed and her hygiene was appropriate, Mandy was just the opposite. When I first met Mandy, there was a slight odor about her; her clothing was disheveled, her makeup was smudged, and her hair was in disarray. She walked into my office, slumped onto my couch, and made very little eye contact with me.

After review of the informed consent and her mother's agreement to waive her rights to Mandy's therapy notes or to be involved in the therapy unless Mandy and I deemed it appropriate, Mandy's mother left the therapy room. As sometimes occurs, Mandy indicated that she did not want to be in therapy and did not believe that she needed therapy, and she would not engage with me. She also stated that "the stupid dogs" were not going to help. I validated Mandy's desire not to be in therapy and gently challenged her idea that she did not need therapy given that she had just been released from a nearby hospital. I asked about that experience. Mandy replied in short sentences, giving little information. At this point, Meika walked over to Mandy, sniffed her, and nudged her hand, as if asking to be petted. Mandy's natural instinct was to reach out and pet Meika. She commented on how soft Meika's fur was and then, realizing what she had done, pulled her hand away and avoided eye contact. Meika then walked over to me and did the same actions. I also responded by petting Meika. At the end of the first session, I indicated that if Mandy could prove to me that she did not need therapy by managing her emotions in healthy ways, was able to refrain from cutting, and acting angrily, then we would not need to see each other for very long. Mandy's curiosity got the better of her, and she asked how long she would need to maintain these behaviors. I replied, "let's see if you can do it for a week."

When Mandy returned the following week, I asked her how her week had been. Mandy reported that it had been "fine." I asked her to explain. During Mandy's explanation, she let it slip that she had gotten into an argument with a girl at school, whom she had hit. Although she had not gotten into trouble with the school over this incident, Mandy admitted she didn't like losing her temper and hitting someone else. When queried about not liking hitting someone, Mandy reported that she had been beaten up at school by a peer and so knew how that felt. I asked Mandy if she might be willing to learn some strategies for holding her temper in check. She begrudgingly said that she would. Over the next several weeks, we practiced many cognitive behavioral techniques for anger management. I also helped Mandy to learn deep breathing, progressive muscle relaxation techniques, and guided imagery relaxation techniques.

As Mandy learned strategies to help contain her anger, she began to trust me and opened up more and more. As is often the case with children and adolescents, she was curious about the therapy dogs. She was talking one day when Meika was sitting near her and licking her fur. Mandy asked why Meika often licked her fur. I indicated that this is how dogs groom to keep themselves clean. Mandy questioned why dogs would want to keep themselves clean. I replied that if dogs are clean, then people are more likely to approach and pay them attention, which is what the therapy dogs enjoy. Mandy laughed and replied, "Well I guess no one will be paying me any attention, will they!" I queried this statement, and Mandy laughed again, suggesting that I look at and perhaps even smell her. We explored the question, if Mandy understood that her hygiene and grooming were important, why would she pay little attention to these things. Eventually, Mandy was able to realize that she used her hygiene and grooming as a defense mechanism to keep people away. Over the next several weeks, we explored why she needed to keep people away and other ways of doing this. As Mandy slowly learned how to use boundaries appropriately with peers and family, her hygiene and grooming improved.

During all this time, Mandy was still cutting. We had attempted to explore this behavior in many different ways; Mandy refused to discuss the issue. One day when I was starting to believe that we were never going to be able to address this issue, Loki came to our rescue. It was summertime, and Loki often experiences allergies during the summer. He was sitting on the couch beside Mandy and chewing at the pads of his feet. I noticed this behavior, apologized to Mandy for the interruption in the session, walked over to Loki, and tried to distract him and stop him from chewing at his feet. Mandy asked why Loki did this. I indicated that he suffers from allergies, and his feet become very itchy. Unfortunately, he sometimes chews them when the itchiness is really bad, and this can cause the pads of his feet to bleed. I indicated that Loki usually takes allergy medication to help him with this problem. This conversation opened the door for Mandy to explore that when she feels so bad and no one is paying attention to her, she cuts to get people's attention. This allowed us to talk about her cutting and how she could use the skills she had already learned to express her feelings in order to seek in healthy ways the attention she needs.

With Mandy better able to manage her emotions, particularly her anger, to use healthy boundaries, and with the improvement in her hygiene and grooming, her self-esteem and confidence also grew. When she discovered appropriate ways to get attention, her cutting stopped completely. When it came time to say good-bye, at our last session, Mandy expressed her gratitude to me and particularly to Meika, Loki, and Hobbes. She indicated that without their loving support and unconditional acceptance, she might not have been able to get better.

Figure 12.2 Meika

Peter: Coping with Depression and Asperger's

Peter was a 16-year-old boy whose parents brought him to see me. Both parents complained that Peter had become increasingly agitated and angry. His mother described situations in which Peter's temper would become uncontrollable, and he would punch holes through walls or break doors off of their hinges. Upon entering the therapy room, Peter immediately went over to Loki, turned to me, and asked the dog's name. Peter ignored me and paid full attention to Loki. Even when I attempted to introduce myself, Peter did not appear interested. This behavior is not unusual for an adolescent who has symptoms of a pervasive developmental disorder.

As is customary in the first session, I went through the informed consent and necessary paperwork. Peter was barely interested. He was talking to and petting Loki. As mentioned above regarding parents waiving their legal right to access the adolescent's therapy notes/information, I again asked for this waiver. When the parents agreed to the waiver, I asked the parents to leave the room.

After Peter's parents left the room, he continued giving his attention to Loki. Nonetheless, I continued with the intake process, and Peter was able to answer questions. I noted that Peter's voice was flat and monotonic. He admitted feeling depressed, agitated, and stressed. I suggested an immediate intervention, and Peter agreed. I suggested that Peter sit on the floor with Loki, place his hand on Loki's belly, and match his breathing to Loki's, which was calm and relaxed. Peter agreed to do this, and after approximately 10 minutes, he reported feeling calmer and less agitated. Even though Peter was comforted by this ability, his body language and tone of voice remained disinterested. We agreed that I would help Peter learn relaxation techniques such as progressive muscle relaxation. The next few weeks of Peter's therapy consisted of me instructing Peter in diaphragmatic breathing, progressive muscle relaxation, and guided visualization relaxation techniques.

Several weeks later, Peter's depression appeared to be worsening. I explored with him the possibility of trying some medication. Peter was ambivalent about it. I explored his ambivalence about taking medications by using the parallel situation of Meika's arthritis. I explained that Meika has arthritis in some of her joints and that she needs to take medication to ease her pain, as her body is unable to produce sufficient pain relief. I explained that Peter's body produced neurotransmitters but wasn't able to use them efficiently and that an antidepressant medication would help the body use the neurotransmitters better. We asked his mother to join the session, and we explored this approach with her. They both agreed to consider it, and if they felt it appropriate, they would call a prescribing doctor and make an appointment.

One day some time later, Peter came into a session and appeared downhearted and despondent. I queried his condition, and he indicated that he wanted to share something with me but was concerned about how to talk about it. We explored what might make it easier for Peter to tell me what he needed to say. He stated that if Meika would join him on the couch, he might feel less anxious about telling me what he wanted to say. So, Peter encouraged Meika to get on the couch with him, which she did. Several minutes later, as Peter petted Meika and looked at me, he related that he had been molested by a friend several years ago. I immediately validated Peter telling me something that was very difficult to say. Peter continued to look at Meika. I sensed Peter's shame and indicated that even though he had told us something very bad that had happened to him, Meika and I believed that Peter was a good boy and that he did not deserve to have been molested. When I suggested that we share this information with his parents, Peter became very agitated, and his voice rose dramatically. Meika reacted to this by jumping down from the couch and coming toward me. Peter was immediately remorseful for scaring Meika, apologized several times, and called her to try to get her to come back to him, which she eventually did. Over the next several weeks, Peter and I explored his feelings and thoughts about having been molested by a friend. Eventually, Peter agreed to allow his mother to join the session so that we could tell her what happened. Needless to say, his mother was shocked that her son had been molested. Peter asked his mother not to tell his father. This request was explored, and we agreed to wait until Peter felt comfortable to ask his father to come to the session so that we could tell him together. Eventually, we were able to tell Peter's father about his being molested. The family explored the possibility of talking to the other boy and his family about the molestation and considered going to the police. They decided to take no action.

Later in Peter's therapy, I suggested that we try to help him learn some important social skills that he appeared not to have gained on his own. For instance, when Peter entered the room, he rarely acknowledged me and would move directly to greet the therapy dog and repeat "good boy, good boy, good boy." I expressed that, typically, most clients say "hello" to me first and then call the therapy dog to them. We practiced how to enter the room, greet me, and then greet the dog one time. He was encouraged to practice saying things only once and to catch himself when repeating a statement.

Finally, Peter's therapy focused on helping him learn to modulate the tone of his voice. Meika was particularly helpful in this vein, as she is very attuned to tone of voice. Hence, Peter was asked to engage with Meika and to ask her to perform certain tricks. If he called her to come and she did not, he was encouraged to change his tone of voice. First, he was encouraged to "sing," that is, to use a slightly higher-pitched voice while uttering the command to come. If she still refused to come, Peter was encouraged to lower his voice to tell her "wrong" and then to sing the command to come. This behavior was practiced over and over in many different situations. Later, Peter was encouraged to use his tone modulation to talk about his feelings, difficult situations, or just for fun. In some cases, he was asked to tell me about a movie he had seen and to use his tone modulation to depict the tension or action in the scene. Hence, if the scene were an action scene, he described it in a rapid and high-pitched voice, whereas if the scene were a dramatic one, he was encouraged to use a low baritone pitch with pauses. Thus, Peter was able to learn how to use voice modulation to depict his feelings or thoughts.

Coco: Establishing the Therapeutic Relationship

I received a phone call from a very distraught mother one day. The mother reported that her 16-year-old daughter had, unbeknownst to her, been cutting her arms several times. The mother tearfully reported that her daughter had expressed self-hatred, was exhibiting behaviors of an eating disorder, and had been cutting for approximately a year. The mother also reported that her daughter had previously been taken to see two therapists. After her daughter had met the therapists for one or two sessions, she refused to continue therapy with either therapist. The mother expressed that I might be her last hope in providing her daughter with the therapeutic help she needed, and so we agreed to meet.

My usual practice for first appointments is to meet with both the parent and adolescent. After going over confidentiality and necessary paperwork, I usually ask the parent to step out of my office if the adolescent feels comfortable so that we can meet one-on-one to discuss the adolescent's concerns. As Coco and her mother entered the room, they were greeted by Loki. Coco immediately sat on the floor with Loki and began to pet him. Coco's mother was a tall, lithe woman, whereas her daughter Coco was of average height and build. After the initial discussion of confidentiality and paperwork, Coco's mother left the room. Coco remained sitting on the floor as she petted Loki. I asked Coco if she had any reactions to what her mother had told me about Coco's eating disorder and her cutting behaviors. Coco agreed with everything her mother had told me. She went on, tearfully, to describe her disgust with several features of her body and how she felt ostracized by her peers at school.

The next week when Coco came to therapy, she was greeted by Hobbes, my Lab mix therapy dog. Hobbes is a true lover in that he will greet most people with kisses galore, and Coco was no exception. She sat on the couch, telling me how her week had been but not mentioning any cutting or eating-disorder behaviors. During this time, I noticed that Hobbes kept nudging Coco's left arm and sniffing under her sleeve. I was just about to ask her about this, when she pulled up her sleeve and showed me several new cuts on her arm. Hobbes's actions allowed Coco to be the one to volunteer the information rather than me having to ask, even though her telling was obviously prompted by Hobbes's actions. Coco stated that she wasn't going to tell me, but she knew that Hobbes knew, and so she felt compelled to tell. She tearfully reported that some girls in her school had casually said something within her hearing about her weight. As she was talking, Hobbes lay beside her, licking her arm and hand, which appeared to help Coco be calm as she continued to report how disgusted she was with herself for being "so fat" and for cutting again. As she continued to pet Hobbes, we explored her thoughts and feelings about this situation and whether she was ready to learn some techniques to help with cutting behaviors. Coco agreed to listen to what I had to say but indicated that she might not agree to try the techniques.

Figure 12.3 Hobbes Teaching Impulse Control

When Coco returned to her session the following week, she appeared a little more upbeat. She indicated that she had used some of the techniques I had provided in her prior session, and they helped. Later, as she continued to explore her perspective regarding her body image, I noticed that as she became more distraught, she reached out for Loki and continued to pet him while she spoke about her negative self-image. At this time, Loki was a little overweight. I queried Coco on what she thought about Loki and his being overweight. Coco said that when she looked at Loki, all she could see was a lovable, happy, wonderful, and accepting dog. She indicated that she didn't see him as being overweight. I paralleled this with Coco's own situation regarding her sense of being overweight and ugly.

Coco's therapy continued like this for several weeks, with me gently challenging Coco's irrational thoughts about herself and, whenever possible, using Loki or Hobbes to help with that process. Some weeks later when Coco reported that she had cut again, we explored her distress on overhearing her school peers giggling and making derogatory comments about her. As she processed her experiences, Hobbes walked over to her and gently nudged her hand, and Coco started to pet Hobbes. As she continued to pet Hobbes and process her experiences, Coco's distress began to subside. She expressed how accepting Hobbes was of her and explored how people can be judgmental and hurtful towards others. She expressed her desire that other humans should be like Hobbes and accept her as she was. During this process, Coco reported that she had been able to connect to me through the therapy dogs. She indicated that the dogs had helped her to feel safe in sharing with me and that both the dogs' and the counselor's nonjudgmental reactions had helped her to see how she was judging herself and others in negative ways.

She reported that her previous therapists had appeared cold, distant, and judgmental and that she viewed me differently primarily because of how I acted with Hobbes and Loki. She was validated for her insights , and the session ended.

With continued weekly therapy, a few months later Coco had stopped cutting, and her self-image had improved. So, we agreed to see each other every other week. Later, the sessions became less frequent, and Coco attended only once a month. Eventually, we agreed to terminate therapy.

Summary

The vignettes above illustrate the therapy dog's power as a co-therapist. The dog might unintentionally create curiosity, which leads to understanding, and might provide safety and comfort , help make the connection between the client and the therapist, and provide the client with support. It is important to note that, had the therapy dog not been present, many of the issues addressed above might not have come to light or might have taken longer to come to light, such as when Mandy saw the dog grooming, which allowed her to understand her defense mechanism. Again, in the story of Coco, given her reluctance to engage in therapy, it seems that the presence of therapy dogs helped to establish the therapeutic relationship and to allow Coco to stay in therapy long enough to learn how to manage her situations.

The vignettes also illustrate that when therapists are competent both in understanding the therapy dog and in their chosen area of work, they can utilize the therapy dogs in ways that help clients manage their anger, develop social skills, learn to self-soothe, learn and use nonverbal behaviors, and parallel the client's life with situations involving the therapy dog.

Figure 12.4 Loki

The orientations most utilized in the above vignettes are person centered, interpersonal process, and object relations. In Mandy's vignette, I also utilized the behavioral therapy, cognitive behavioral therapy, and attachment orientations. Behavioral and cognitive behavioral therapy were illustrated when Mandy was introduced to and learned deep breathing, progressive muscle relaxation techniques, and guided imagery relaxation techniques. Both Mandy's and Coco's vignettes had some aspects of attachment orientation in the process. Both girls were distressed by their lack of attachment with peers, and in Mandy's case, with her family. Coco's vignette also includes aspects of the psychodynamic and cognitive orientations. Specifically, I used the cognitive orientation when I challenged her irrational thoughts about herself. Moreover, the psychodynamic orientation was present in Coco's vignette when the therapy dogs brought to light her unconscious desire to be accepted and loved unconditionally, not judged; of course, this approach is also an aspect of the person-centered orientation. In working with Peter, I used both solution-focused brief therapy and emotionally focused work.

Chapter
13

Animal-Assisted Psychotherapy Interventions with Adults

According to many authors, animal-assisted psychotherapy (AAP) can be beneficial for many people, including adults. In addition, as stated in previous chapters, AAP can be helpful in treating adults with mental illnesses, such as anxiety disorders, mood disorders, anger problems, and attachment issues and can assist in developing insight and many other treatment issues. Adults who are animal lovers might tend to be more acceptable of AAP. Nonetheless, even those who are not animal lovers can still benefit from AAP.

The following case vignettes involving adults demonstrate the modality of AAP in planned interventions focused on managing anger, developing social skills, learning to self-soothe, paralleling a dog's experience with clients' experiences to aid in achieving goals regarding medication and grooming, and learning how to identify and use nonverbal behaviors. The vignettes also demonstrate how AAP can work in unplanned interventions, such as using clients' curiosity regarding the dog to understand their own defenses or the purpose of their attention-seeking behaviors, providing safety and comfort for disclosure of difficult material, how the therapy dog aids in establishing the therapeutic alliance, how the therapy dog inadvertently encourages the disclosure of self-harming behaviors, and how clients receive comfort from the therapy dog.

Deborah: The Practice of Being Seen and Not Heard

Deborah was a middle-aged woman who was self-referred for therapy. Her cause of concern was a shocking level of anger that she had begun experiencing in her marital relationship. Deborah had agreed to AAP, as she already knew the healing power of dogs in her personal life. Loki, my loving collie mix, was working with us one day. He had lain beside Deborah's feet. She was processing a recent experience with anger , when she moved to recross one of her legs. The sudden movement startled Loki, and he quickly stood up to see what had happened. Deborah's reaction was surprising as she became very agitated and upset that she had "startled" Loki. She immediately became almost childlike in her attempt to appease and calm Loki, who was still calm. She apologized profusely for "upsetting" him and then burst into tears. In processing her reaction to Loki and her projection of "upsetting" him, she identified her "learned" behavior of "being seen and not heard" and not being allowed to express her feelings, as they were often "stuffed and forgotten."

Figure 13.1 Meika at 6 months

This moment and subsequent sessions allowed Deborah to connect with her feelings and "learned" behaviors. Of course, this dynamic was currently playing out in her marital relationship. Her husband had made some important decisions for them without first discussing them with Deborah. To help Deborah with this, we agreed to try some role-plays focused on how she could assert herself. Deborah found the empty chair technique "silly." So, we agreed to have Loki sit in the chair opposite her and for her to assert her needs to her husband. During this process, I encouraged Loki to "speak," or bark. Deborah was encouraged to hear this as her husband talking against her needs and for her to continue asserting her needs. We practiced this technique for a few sessions until Deborah was able to talk over Loki's barking and finish her part of the conversation with her husband, despite being interrupted.

A month later, Deborah was able to have the conversation with her husband, who was surprised and surprisingly receptive to her thoughts about the situation. They resolved the misunderstanding and began a new part of their relationship, in which her husband would discuss things with Deborah.

Melanie: Unresolved Grief

Melanie was referred for court-ordered therapy. Needless to say, her engagement was less than what one would appreciate or require for therapeutic progress. She came regularly to her weekly appointments and used the time to "vent" her anger against the system that was making her attend something she clearly did not think she needed. She reluctantly agreed to allow me to use AAP and appeared completely uninterested in connecting with the therapist or the co-therapist dog Meika.

Several weeks into therapy and only a few weeks before she could terminate, given that the court had ordered her to attend therapy for 10 weeks, Melanie mentioned that she had a dog when she was a young girl. I asked what happened to the dog, and Melanie reported that the dog had died of cancer. To Melanie's surprise, she began to cry. Meika noticed this behavior, got up, crossed the room, and put her head in Melanie's lap. As Melanie petted Meika, she described how much she had loved her dog, Rufus, and missed him. She continued to gently cry as she explored her unresolved grief for her beloved pet.

The following week Melanie returned to therapy with a more positive attitude toward us. She smiled as she greeted us and reported a "good week." I checked in concerning the last session and any thoughts or reactions Melanie might have had to the session. Melanie described how she had pulled out photos of "her Rufus" and noted that her deceased father was in many of the photos with Rufus. She had forgotten how connected the three of them were. At this point, she called Meika to her and asked me if Meika could join her on the couch. I agreed, and Meika joined Melanie on the couch. As Melanie petted Meika, she relayed how her father had died a few years earlier. Again, as she sobbed gently, it was apparent that Melanie had unresolved grief related to her father's passing as well. We continued to process her grief and loss over the next several weeks, with Meika's ever-gentle presence beside Melanie as a comfort to her.

Melanie continued therapy for several months after her court-appointed time had expired. When she terminated counseling, Melanie indicated that she had fully intended to come only for the 10 weeks the court had ordered her to complete. She further indicated that she had not thought that therapy would benefit her but that now she saw how much it benefitted her and lifted the weight of her unresolved grief for the death of both her father and her beloved pet. She stated that she would return if she felt the need at some future time.

Christine: How the Dog Co-Therapist Brings the Client Back to Therapy after a Clinical Fracture

Christine, a 40-year-old woman came to us after she had been "abandoned" by her current therapist. She was angry and wary of beginning a new therapeutic relationship but was also smart enough to realize that she was not sufficiently emotionally stable to be okay without therapy.

An American family had adopted Christine from an foreign orphanage. Her adoptive family had tried to mold her into the "cute little girl" they wanted instead of accepting the tomboy they had. This molding used emotions and both physical and sexual abuse to control her behaviors. She had told a therapist of her abuse around age nine, but the therapist had not believed her and told her parents. They, of course, punished her for lying. So, Christine eventually started to drink and run away from home. She continued drinking for 25 years.

Christine came to us with four years of sobriety and after having been hospitalized three times. She was chronically depressed and often suicidal. Not surprisingly given the years of abuse she had experienced, she was also emotionally delayed. Christine was an animal lover, particularly a dog lover. She immediately connected with Meika and Loki and later with Hobbes.

Figure 13.2 Loki

In the past, I had chosen a particular dog to work with a particular client to help focus on specific treatment issues, but clients often asked to meet the other dog, and as Meika and Loki have very different temperaments, they allow for different foci for therapy. I have since alternated the dogs with all clients so that in one week, Meika will come on Monday and Wednesday and Loki on Tuesday and Thursday. The following week, they rotate so that Loki comes Monday and Wednesday and Meika on Tuesday and Thursday. Later, after Meika retired, Hobbes alternated with Loki, using the same rotations.

Hence, Christine was able to connect with all the dogs and, through them, to the therapist. Much later, as part of Christine's therapy treatment, she agreed to learn the skills of Dialectical Behavior Therapy (DBT). In a section of the DBT skills, the client and I work on challenging myths related to emotions. In this particular exercise, the counselor attempts to challenge the client's "facts" about emotions, which are often erroneous, in order to develop challenges to these purported facts. During this process, I challenged each of Christine's myths related to her emotions. During the second session in which these challenges occurred, Christine became angry with me. She stated that if I insisted on threatening her belief structure in this way that she would terminate therapy. Although I attempted to minimize the fracture of the safety that I had painstakingly developed, Christine remained angry and left the session. Later that week Christine called me and left a message that she would not return for therapy. I retuned her call and asked that she attend a "termination" session to attempt to resolve the fracture and/or to say good-bye, particularly to one of the therapy dogs. Christine agreed.

When Christine returned for her "termination" session, she began explaining how angry she had been and queried why I had not stopped pushing her to give up her beliefs. I apologized for underestimating the level of Christine's anger and confusion related to the myths that I was challenging. As this was occurring, Loki, my 75-pound collie mix, jumped on the couch and started to nudge Christine and lick her arm. Christine asked me why Loki was behaving this way. I asked Christine why she thought he would act this way. Christine stated that maybe Loki knew how upset she was and was trying to help her feel better. I agreed that this might be true. Christine also wondered if Loki was also trying to tell her to stay. I asked if this was something she was considering, and Christine indicated that she wanted to stay so she could spend time with Loki and Meika but that she was still angry with me for not seeing her distress.

Over the next few months Christine continued her therapy, and through her relationship with Meika, Loki, and later Hobbes, she reestablished the safety of the therapeutic relationship and continued to use what she learned about repairing relationships in her life.

Tiffany: Learning to Recognize Her Own Emotional States

We first met Tiffany after she had been released from a local inpatient treatment program. Tiffany had been in the program due to her cutting behaviors. This last treatment program was one of many hospitalizations. I received a call from her partner asking if I would be willing to meet with Tiffany and the partner for a consultation. As is my custom, I asked if they were willing to have a dog present for the consultation, and they agreed. I offer a free, 15-minute consultation by phone or in person so that people can determine whether they believe they would be comfortable working with the therapy dogs and me. So far, I have never had anyone who has come to a consultation choose not to work with us.

Tiffany, a 30-something woman, came to us with a history replete with physical, emotional, and sexual trauma throughout her life. She also had a past history of alcohol and drug abuse. Unsurprisingly, she had difficulty with feeling safe, her emotions, and connecting with others. It was very evident that Tiffany experienced high states of anxiety and distress while talking about routine experiences.

During the 15-minute consultation, Tiffany asked questions about my trauma training and how the dogs are involved in the treatment. I answered her questions as Meika introduced herself and accepted petting from Tiffany and her partner. During our meeting, it was obvious that Tiffany was connecting to Meika and to me. She was even able to laugh, something her partner stated she had not done in some time.

So, Tiffany, Loki, Meika, Hobbes, and I began our trauma work. My trauma work is based on Judith Herman's seminal work on trauma: Trauma and Recovery. I use the three-phase model for trauma work: 1) establishing safety with self and others; 2) reprocessing the trauma; and 3) connecting back to life and loved ones in healthy adaptive patterns. I knew, even from the 15-minute consultation, that much of our initial work would focus on establishing safety for Tiffany.

At some point in the first phase of Tiffany's treatment, it was apparent that she often dissociated and was unaware of what she was feeling. This behavior was clearly demonstrated one day when Loki, wanting to be a lap dog, jumped up on the couch and started gently pawing Tiffany. She was exploring a recent experience in which she was afraid and anxious. As she relayed her story, Loki became more and more determined to touch Tiffany. He was on the couch, trying to crawl onto her lap. I asked her to stop her story and to go inside and see what was occurring for her. She relayed that her heart was racing, her breathing was rapid, and she felt flushed. When asked what her emotion was, Tiffany was unable to identify it. Nevertheless, as she petted Loki, she reported her heart slowing, her breathing becoming more regular, and her skin returning to normal temperature.

At other times in Tiffany's work as she explored current situations that upset her, she was unable to recall important aspects of the events. When queried about her physical state at the time, she was able to identify that her heart was racing, her breathing was rapid, and she felt flushed. We continued to explore this phenomenon many times. Every time this happened in session, if Loki was present, he would immediately go to Tiffany and attempt to connect with her. He was often very insistent in his attention, pawing and licking Tiffany for up to 10 minutes. Over time, Tiffany discovered that these physical symptoms occurred just prior to her dissociating and that Loki was attempting to ground her. With this knowledge, Tiffany was better prepared to cope and to manage her dissociations.

Later in Tiffany's safety work, she came to one of her sessions in an apparent state of agitation. She indicated that she had a "near miss" in her vehicle because she had been "absorbed" in her thoughts. When I asked Tiffany how she was doing, she indicated that she was scared, anxious, and upset. She also reported a racing heart, trembling, difficulty breathing, fearing that she was going to lose control, and some nausea. I indicated that she appeared to be in the beginning of a panic attack, which Tiffany agreed she was. I suggested to her that she place her hand on Loki's belly and that she match her breathing to his . While she matched her breathing to Loki's, I spoke calmly and slowly to her, telling her that she was going to be okay and that she could make it through this panic attack. After several minutes, Tiffany reported that her panic attack symptoms had subsided, and she felt calm again. Whenever

Tiffany reported that she was beginning to experience a panic attack, she would be encouraged to practice the behaviors described above. She performed this technique several times throughout the therapy.

Figure 13.3 Loki Helping Ameliorate a Panic Attack

A year later, Tiffany returned from vacation and happily reported to me that while she was on vacation, she had successfully averted two panic attacks. After validating her success, I asked how she had accomplished such an amazing feat. She reported that when she had noticed a panic attack beginning, she had visualized being in my office, sitting with Loki, and matching her breathing to his. She smiled as she told me that this visualization helped her to remember how to change her breathing and calm herself when she experienced panic attack symptoms. Tiffany stated that she was happy she had learned this technique and that now she knew that she could successfully manage her panic attacks without use of medications.

Typically, when Tiffany enters my therapy room, she will walk over to my couch, put her bag on the floor, sit down, and immediately call the furry facilitator to her. She often spends at least five minutes talking to and petting the furry facilitator. She asks the dogs how they are doing and will sometimes comment on whether they look happy or sad. Eventually, she will turn her gaze to me and acknowledge my presence. Tiffany often comments that she feels accepted by my therapy dogs and also by me. Sometimes, when she makes such comments, this will allow her to acknowledge the loss of acceptance she experienced in childhood by her parents and the message that she was an "awful child." In this way, the furry facilitator brought to light the irrational thoughts regarding Tiffany being an "awful child." I could then challenge Tiffany's splitting and defenses in a compassionate, empathic, "good mother" role.

Rachel: Grounding Dissociative Processes

Rachel, a 30-something woman, was self-referred to me. She indicated that she had been in therapy for more than a year with a therapist but did not feel that the work was productive. Rachel reported a significant history of emotional, physical, and sexual abuse from an early age. As usual, I explained the three phases of trauma treatment: 1) stabilization; 2) reprocessing; and 3) reintegration to life. Even though she had been in therapy for almost a year, she had very few coping skills related to flashbacks, intrusive images and thoughts, and/or disassociation. So, we began with the stabilization phase.

During the stabilization phase, Rachel reported hearing voices. When I assessed this, the voices were internal to her. She reported hearing voices of different people; some were children, some were adolescents, and others were adults. It was at this point that I tentatively diagnosed dissociative identity disorder. Rachel had a hard time believing that she had several alters who held memories of her traumas. As is typical in the initial treatment of dissociative identity disorder, we focused on establishing communication and collaboration between the different parts.

During a particularly difficult session for Rachel, she disassociated, but no alter came to the forefront. Even though Rachel was dissociated and her eyes were defocused, she reported being in a dark cellar. I used typical grounding techniques, such as asking Rachel to look around her and name things that she could see, hear, smell, or physically feel in the therapy room. Rachel was unable to perform this process. It was at this time that I asked Rachel if she could bring Hobbes over to her, sit him on the couch beside her, and reach out and touch him. Rachel agreed, indicating that she was scared, as the place was dark and cold. I had Hobbes lie on the couch next to Rachel and instructed her to put her hand out directly in front of her. At this point, Hobbes sniffed her hand and then began to lick her. This immediately brought Rachel out of her dissociative process and back into the present day. This dissociative process occurred several times for Rachel, and I was able to successfully bring her back to the present by having Rachel touch the therapy dog or allowing the therapy dog to lick her.

Once Rachel had become sufficiently stable and had established communication and collaboration with several of her alters, we began to engage the alters to reprocess their experiences and to share them with Rachel. This process, of course, was done very slowly over a period of several years. As homework, Rachel was often assigned the task of allowing an alter to journal or depict his or her trauma through artwork. During sessions Rachel was asked to explore the artwork or to read from the journal. During these times Rachel was encouraged to practice grounding techniques and progressive muscle relaxation. It was notable that Rachel often attempted during these times to have the therapy dog sit beside her to keep herself grounded or to help ease her distressing emotions. If disassociation were noted, I would redirect Rachel to focus on the therapy dog beside her and to follow the dog's breathing pattern. This action would help to ground Rachel and to re-stabilize her emotional process.

Occasionally, when Rachel entered the therapy room, she paid particular attention to the therapy dog. In these instances, I could tell after some time whether Rachel or one of her alters was present based on the way she treated the therapy dog. As is typical, I always provide space for the client and the therapy dog to greet each other and for the client to feel comforted by the therapy dog. It is not unusual for a client to spend several minutes saying "hi" to the therapy dog before the client acknowledges me. I think this behavior indicates a level of connection that clients often feel toward the therapy dogs. Clients also typically say good-bye to the therapy dog at the end of the session.

In one session, Rachel was particularly distraught and was expressing suicidal ideation. She had recently lost someone she felt close to and safe with but was avoiding dealing with her grief. She expressed a desire to be with the loved one who had died. During this process, I asked what her thoughts were, and what, if any, plan she had for taking her life. She indicated that she was overwhelmed by feelings of sadness and wanting to be with her loved one. When queried further about any plan for suicide, Rachel indicated that she had not formulated a plan. As she spoke these words, Loki sat up and tilted his head to one side. Rachel looked at me and back to Loki and then said, "he doesn't believe me, does he?" Before I could say anything, Rachel expressed that no one ever believed her. In prior sessions, when Rachel had learned from an alter about a particular aspect of her abuse, she often expressed difficulty believing what they had shared with her. I asked Rachel if she was stating that Loki did not believe her when really she was unable to believe that she felt this desperate to take her own life. At this point, Rachel started to cry. As she sobbed through her tears, she expressed a deep experience of loneliness, sadness, hopelessness, worthlessness, and that she was not cared for by anyone. This has continued to be a large part of Rachel's process in her therapy.

In some cases, the client/alter often has a preference for one of the therapy dogs, which is the case with Rachel. Rachel openly expressed fond affection for Hobbes, the youngest of my therapy dogs and the one that acts most like a puppy. In exploring this attraction, Rachel was able to identify that Hobbes was always happy to see her, always wanted to give her "kisses," and accepted her completely, even when another alter was present. This behavior was in stark contrast to her own childhood upbringing and led Rachel to explore numerous experiences of being rejected and feeling unloved, unwanted, and unworthy. Through Hobbes's unconditional love and complete acceptance, Rachel was able to start feeling loved, wanted, and worthy.

Summary

These vignettes show the power of my furry facilitators as they foster attachment, safety and comfort, connection between the client and the therapist, and insight. I believe that in some of these experiences, had the furry facilitator not been present, some of the issues addressed above might not have come to light or might have taken longer to come to light.

The planned interventions described in the previous pages facilitated clients' learning assertiveness, decreasing anxiety, preventing panic attacks from occurring, exploring grief and loss, and assisting in grounding themselves when dissociated. Unplanned interventions facilitated by the animal co-therapists led to insight, the processing of family dynamics, resolving grief or loss, and repairing attachment injuries.

In all of the vignettes above, we can easily see the orientations of person centered, interpersonal process, and emotion focused. Additionally, in the vignette concerning Deborah, we can see the orientations of person centered,

EFT, and cognitive behavioral. Similarly, in Melanie's vignette, we can also see the psychodynamic and object relations orientations. In Christine's vignette, we can see the additional orientations of attachment, object relations, and psychodynamic. With Tiffany, the other orientations demonstrated include attachment, object relations, cognitive behavioral, and psychodynamic. The vignette concerning Rachel's treatment also includes the cognitive behavioral, attachment, object relations, and psychodynamic orientations.

Chapter
14

Family Therapy Facilitated by Therapy Dogs

Working with families can be challenging for many therapists. This can be particularly true when issues of trauma are involved. Some authors claim that the presence of a therapy dog can create a family-systems phenomenon known as triangulation, that projection, displacement, and identification can occur, and that family dynamics can be played out with the furry facilitator. Authors have also indicated that the animal co-therapist's presence can create a sense of safety, calmness, and help to build rapport and trust. Moreover, authors have suggested that people may moderate their behavior in the presence of the animal co-therapist and that the animal's misbehavior can help parents learn to manage children's misbehavior when the therapist role-models appropriate correction of the animal's behavior. Finally, these authors have suggested that the animals may act as a catalyst for the discussion of deep-rooted emotional difficulties.[1]

In the two vignettes presented below, the planned interventions include building rapport, safety, and trust. The furry facilitators act as transitional aspects of objects to facilitate these interventions. Other planned interventions include processing feelings, learning to be calm, and processing loss. The unplanned interventions in these two vignettes include identifying projection, building self-esteem, anger management, learning coping skills, exploring traumatic experiences, and processing feelings of exclusion.

A Family Torn Apart by Domestic Violence and Substance Abuse

The Kelly family was referred to me by a colleague who was working with the mother. The mother was experiencing domestic violence in her relationship with her husband, which the children were witnessing and beginning to experience themselves. The Kelly family had three young children, two girls and a boy, all under the age of 8. I will refer to the oldest girl as Susie and her younger sister as Jane. The boy I will call Andy. As is sometimes the case, I met with the mother first. She indicated that her husband was verbally abusive and drinking excessively. She denied any physical violence towards her or the children. As is usual with informed consent, I went over the boundaries of

---

[1] Chandler (2005, 2012); Fine (2010); Walsh (2009).

confidentiality and explained that, if the children were to report to me that they fear being physically assaulted by their father or are in fact assaulted by him, I would need to call child protective services. The mother indicated that she understood.

Figure 14.1 Loki Playing

Initially, I agreed to work with the two older girls, as the youngest boy was not showing any signs of stress or impact from the verbal abuse in the marriage. The mother reported that the girls were reacting differently to the abuse they were hearing. One daughter, Susie, was becoming more withdrawn, isolated, and moody, whereas the other, Jane, was openly expressing her fears , sadness, and anger. As usual, the therapy dogs were wonderful transitional objects. The girls immediately attached to Loki, Meika, and through them, to me. Within a few sessions, the girls were opening up and telling me what was happening in their home. Shortly after I began working with the family, both girls reported that their father was drinking wine while driving. When queried on how they knew it was wine, both girls reported they had seen their father pouring from a bottle of wine into a flask that he uses to drink while driving. At this point, I asked the girls to leave and the mother to join the session. I informed the mother of what had just been reported to me and told the mother she would be calling Child Protective Services.

Some time later, Susie, who had been withdrawn, isolated, and moody, was encouraged by me to write about her feelings in a journal that I provided. She was told that she would not have to share this journal with me or with her mother if she did not want to. During a later session, Susie asked to meet with me alone. She indicated that she had written some things in the journal that she would like to share with Meika. I encouraged her to do this. Susie read excerpts from her journal that described her seeing her father hitting her mother. As she explored the confusion and anger , I noticed Meika pawing at Susie. I reflected Meika's actions as trying to console or comfort Susie. Susie threw her arms around Meika's neck and began to sob. I reflected the sadness Susie felt about seeing her mother being hurt. Susie was also able to identify feeling scared. This interaction allowed me the opportunity to work on safety issues in this particular situation. Susie and I explored ways that Susie could remain safe, such as going to her bedroom or locking herself in the bathroom while her parents were arguing and fighting. She was also encouraged to take her siblings with her so that they could stay together. Susie and I determined what types of activities they could do when they were together in a safe place. Susie and I agreed that activities that would be helpful to all of the children included reading to each other, drawing together, using a coloring book, and/or playing some nice music. Susie was encouraged to share these ideas with Jane so that they would both know what to do when their parents started arguing and so that they could help their brother Andy feel safer.

After the father was removed from the home, Andy started having temper tantrums. He then started family therapy with his two older siblings. One of the rules I explain to children when I start working with them is that they are not allowed to hurt the therapy dogs. Andy, of course, agreed to this stipulation. Later in another therapy session, Andy started becoming angry. He was missing his father and was angry that his father was taken away from him. Andy started to raise his voice; as his voice got louder, Loki became uncomfortable and moved away from him. Andy reacted to Loki's moving away by becoming upset and starting to cry. Andy wanted to know why Loki didn't like him. I explained to Andy that Loki liked Andy very much but that Andy's tone of voice was frightening to Loki, which is why he was moving away. I assured Andy that if he could calm down, use a friendly tone of voice, and smile that Loki would come back and sit beside him again. Initially, Andy found it difficult to calm himself, so we practiced pretending to blow bubbles. Using this technique, Andy was encouraged to breathe deeply and calm himself down. Once he was calmer, he was able to call Loki in a gentle voice. Loki, of course, came back to sit with Andy again.

Andy and I explored Loki's reaction to Andy's loud voice. Using a parallel process technique, I paralleled Loki's reaction to Andy's shouting with Andy's own experience of hearing his father shout at his mother. I validated Andy's feelings of being scared and upset. Andy was then able to express that he wanted his parents to speak to each other calmly, just as he had done with Loki. I then also paralleled what Loki did to help himself feel safe and okay in that Loki left Andy and went over to the corner of the room to his safe place. I encouraged Andy to consider a safe place for him in his home that he could go to when his parents were arguing or fighting. His sisters, Susie and Jane, suggested that they all go to the bedroom or the bathroom, where they could draw, color, play a game, or listen to some music together. Andy agreed that this was a good idea.

Figure 14.2 Hobbes Playing

Later, due to issues of insurance changing, the family could no longer continue working with us. They were provided with an appropriate referral to an agency that could meet their needs and that took their new health insurance. Each of the children asked to say good-bye to both Loki and Meika As I alternate the dogs every week, termination or saying good-bye takes at least two weeks. Susie expressed that because Loki loves treats, she wanted to bring him a nice treat. We agreed that was a good way to say good-bye to Loki. As for Meika, Susie chose to bring her a small bottle of bubbles, as this activity was their favorite game together. Jane chose to say good-bye to both Meika and Loki by asking them to give her one last hug. Andy chose to say good-bye to both dogs by leaving them with a picture of him and his siblings, so the dogs would remember them.

A Family Working through Separation and Divorce

The Richards family came to me after their mother had left the family unexpectedly. The family consisted of the father, Peter, two sons, Edwin and Charles, and the youngest sibling, a girl, Rosemary. As the Richards family came into the therapy room, all children immediately gravitated towards Loki, who was lying in the corner of the room. Peter knew that I was an animal-assisted psychotherapist, but he immediately acted to protect his children from this unknown dog. He asked his children to leave the dog alone and to sit on the couch with him, which they reluctantly did. As I completed the introductions and went through the paperwork and informed consent discussion, the children's questions were directed to me regarding Loki. Loki's presence appeared to put the children at ease. Even though they had come to see me under upsetting circumstances, i.e., their mother leaving them, they were able to laugh, smile, and appeared relaxed and at ease in the therapy setting. I explained to the children that when they had completed an assigned task during the session, they would then be allowed to play with Loki or whatever dog was present for the session.

In the next session, I indicated that all of the therapy dogs were trained to do specific tricks. Once the children had completed their therapeutic tasks, they were then encouraged one at time to engage with the therapy dog and to encourage the dog to perform a trick. Thus, after exploring their negative feelings regarding their mother's absence, they were then allowed to engage the therapy dog, which resulted in their feelings being processed, which in turn fostered a positive relationship to the therapy.
So, for the next 12 weeks, the children came to the sessions, checked in on the past week's events, and their experiences were validated by me. We then engaged in a specific activity related to children going through a divorce. Once the children had completed the activity, they were then allowed to interact with the therapy dog.

As often occurs in family or group work, the therapist might find it difficult to pay specific attention to everyone. Nonetheless, this can illuminate the family dynamics or a family member's internal processes. Often, in particular paid more attention to the two boys than to the little girl, Rosemary. At these times, Rosemary attempted to get closer to me. In one particular session, the two boys were petting Loki, and Rosemary came over and sat on my lap. I noted the interaction, and Rosemary was able to explore her sense of exclusion, not just in the therapy room but also at home with the boys, who often played together and did not want to play with her. After her feelings were validated, we explored what she might be able to do to engage with the boys when they are playing together at home. This process also allowed Rosemary to express her sadness at her mother's departure. Rosemary explained that at times, the boys had refused to allow her to play with them, so she would often go spend time with her mother. Of course, with Rosemary expressing her sadness, this discussion also allowed the boys to explore their feelings of sadness and anger regarding their mother leaving them.

During a later session, Edwin, the oldest son, was attempting to have Meika perform the "stick 'em up" trick. When Meika refused to cooperate, Edwin indicated that sometimes his friends at school refused to play with him. Instead of focusing on the peer relationship issue, I refocused back on Meika and why she might not want to play with Edwin. Edwin was able to identify a few reasons why Meika would not engage with him, such as she was tired, she wasn't feeling well, or she didn't want to do that specific trick but might be willing to do another trick. I was then able to parallel Edwin's thoughts to his peer relationship issue. Thus, Edwin was able to feel better about himself regarding his friends not wanting to play with him and had ideas about how to re-engage his peers.

In another session activity, the children explored their feelings related to their mother leaving and their parents getting divorced. This process encouraged the children to express their feelings. Charles, at this time, was very angry about his mother leaving them. While each child shared their feelings, Loki was lying off to the side of the office away from me. When Charles explored his anger, his voice was tense and became louder. When this happened,

Loki got up, sniffed at Charles, and came to sit by me. I reflected that Loki was uncomfortable with Charles's expression of anger and sought to be comforted by me. This process allowed Charles to see the impact of his anger on Loki. A short while later, Charles became calmer and indicated that he was really sad about his mother leaving and thought that she did not love him. At this time, Loki got up from beside me, walked across the room, sat next to Charles, and licked him. I expressed that Loki could sense Charles's sadness and was trying to show him what a nice boy he was and that he was lovable. With this event, Charles openly cried, and his brother, sister, father, and Loki all had a group hug.

A few weeks later, it was time to terminate therapy with the family. At this time, the clients were not saying good-bye only to the therapist, but they also needed time to say good-bye to the therapy dog. We began planning termination for a few weeks so the children would be able to say good-bye to both therapy dogs, Meika and Loki. Typically, I allow children to determine how they choose to say good-bye to the therapy dogs. The Richards children all had their own ideas about how they wanted to say good-bye to Meika and Loki. Edwin and Charles both chose to bring Loki a special treat, knowing what a food-oriented dog he is. Rosemary wanted Loki to do all of his tricks for her, so the treats her brothers brought were very helpful in gaining Loki's cooperation. They all chose to say good-bye to Meika by receiving a hug from her and each spending a few minutes of one-on-one time to pet her and say good-bye. I suggested that they might want to also draw a picture of the dogs and to write something special that each dog had taught them about themselves. Edwin's drawing stated that he had learned he was a "good kid"; Charles's drawing stated that "he knew he was loved," and Rosemary's drawing stated that she "was special too."

Summary

As far as I can see, the power of my furry facilitators is limitless. Just when you think you've seen it all, they do something unique that allows clients to work through issues and attain a better quality of life. Sometimes these benefits occur inadvertently, such as when Rosemary sat on my lap. Others happen in a planned manner. As shown in the previous vignettes, the animal co-therapist often acts as a transitional object or object for attachment; the therapy dogs foster safety and comfort , connection between the client and the therapist, and insight. Although most of these issues would have come into the therapy room eventually, I believe it is likely that these happen sooner because of the presence of my furry facilitators.

Planned interventions as described in the previous pages include building rapport, safety, and trust, assisting in calming, and the processing of loss and grief as well as difficult emotions or beliefs about the self. Unintentional interventions occur when the client reacts to the animal co-therapist, or the animal co-therapist does something that elicits a dynamic for the client. In the vignettes described in this chapter, we can see that the unintentional interventions fostered sharing, projection, closure, issues of self-esteem, and management of anger. When the animal co-therapist acts instantaneously to a stimulus, such as a raised voice, this behavior allows me to intervene immediately in using the animal's reaction as a safe way to explore the dynamic that just occurred.

In both of the family therapy vignettes presented above, one can see my use of the interpersonal process, person-centered, cognitive behavioral therapy, emotion-focused, play therapy, and psychodynamic orientations. Moreover, in the Kelly family sessions, one can also see the use of the object relations and attachment theory orientations. In the Richards family sessions, one can see the additional use of cognitive therapy, such as when I asked Edwin to consider other reasons why Meika would not perform the trick he had requested of her.

Chapter
15

Client Reflections on Animal-Assisted Psychotherapy

The following are past client reflections on animal-assisted psychotherapy (AAP). These reflections are from children, adolescents, adults, and families, and they illustrate how wonderful and powerful AAP is from clients' perspectives.

I have long appreciated the love and acceptance of animals and have sought them out when suffering from bouts of depression. I had a pet dog for 18 years and she sensed when I was sick or depressed. She would look at me with her soulful eyes as if to say "I understand" and she would sit at/on my feet or curl up next to me on the couch and just "be" with me. Her warm body comforted me and the act of petting relaxed my anxiety. So when I was looking for a therapist, at a very difficult time in my life, I was happy to learn about animal assisted therapy offered by Dr. Lynn Piper. Her dogs were so accepting and calming. They brought a smile to my face when I felt I hadn't smiled for days. They were big, furry, friendly dogs. They were clean and did not have an odor either - just like big stuffed animals come to life! I could pet them or not. They were well behaved and not needy but at the same time responsive. They were good listeners too. I looked forward to my appointments more because of the dogs.

Adult Female

Due to a very unfortunate event August 8, 2009, I found myself in a situation to seek family counseling for my three children. The trust in their mother was taken from them when she left the house for a scout meeting and unbeknownst to us had no intention of returning. Some weeks later, she found it necessary to tell the children that she had left them to marry a family friend and scout leader who left this wife and three children as well to be with their mother. I give this background information to help you understand the grave lack of trust bestowed upon my children from adults in their lives who were supposed to love them unconditionally and/or have their best interest at heart in reverence to

God. In an effort to help them deal with the trauma of the abandonment by their mother, they find themselves in the car on the way to an adult authority figure, that they do not know, who is going to help them understand why people who said that they loved them abandoned them. This was a traumatic car ride for me and I can only imagine the anxiety within my children. I was instructed to let my children know that the doctor had a dog that they could play with once we arrived. We have a wonderful dog at home and this initially helped ease the tears as to why they needed to go see this adult doctor in regards to how they feel. Upon arriving to the office building and entering the waiting room, I could tell the children's emotions and fears were welling up inside of them. I am certain they were thinking, how is talking to this adult authority figure going to help me understand why my mom abandoned me. Well, the angst ended when the kids walked down the hall, opened the door to a beautiful dog wagging his tail at them. They asked could they pet him to which permission was immediately granted. After everyone had petted, hugged and kissed our new canine friend, the task at hand seemed effortless. The ice had been broken and hearts softened. They knew that there are adults that are here to help. On the way home, my kids smiled, laughed and wanted to know when they could go back to see Dr. Piper and her dog. Over the many months of our sessions, my kids could not wait to go see Dr. Piper and her two dogs. I truly believe that my children. were open to talking to an adult about their feelings and what happened to them because of the loving effects of Dr. Piper's dogs. Given the distrust they had for their mother and adults in authority, I believe if I had taken my children to a sterile, hospital type environment for their therapy, we would not have had such a successful result. Today, I have three wonderful, happy children. Thank you!

A Family

Animal assisted therapy was such a soft place to go for the children and I to fall since we were suffering through such a traumatic experience. We had always loved animals, especially dogs. They just give love and "listen" without judgment. They also allow the "ice" to be broken and they bring/give such peace and calm. By lessening the immediate stress of a person, it allows the therapist to provide guidance and therapy. It also adds an additional motivation to attend therapy sessions, especially with kids due to their desire to "have fun". I see this as similar to play therapy, which allows children to work through issues or experiences and for the therapist to get at difficult subjects "through a different or back door.

A Mother

As a woman in her early 40s with trust and abandonment issues, I sought help from Dr. Piper. Being an animal lover, I was intrigued by the concept of animal assisted therapy. During my initial intake, my anxiety quickly disappeared when I met Loki, a 70 lb. mutt. He was so excited to meet a new friend and I decided that if Loki was okay then Dr. Piper must be okay as well.

As Dr. Piper, her dogs, and I worked together over several years, I developed better trust, self-confidence and tools to manage my abandonment issues. Thanks to the presence of animals, my personal growth was cultivated in a very safe and soothing environment. Having Loki, Mika and Hobbs present during my therapy sessions provided me with a sense of trust, unconditional love, comfort, dependability and companionship as I explored some very difficult areas in my life. There were many times I did not want to go to my therapy session, but because I wanted to see Loki and his incredible positive energy and bright spirit, I showed up for my appointment despite the anxiety. My experience with animal assisted therapy was very rewarding; it gave me the foundation to work through my personal issues and helped me to become a stronger person.

Adult Female

Dog Therapy

When I was with the dogs they made me feel good, because I have a dog and it made me feel comfortable. Mrs. Piper was awsome because she made me feel like it's okay to only live with my daddy, because alot of people only live with one of the parents. I love you Mrs. Piper!!!♡☺

A Young Girl

Chapter 16

Final Reflections on Animal-Assisted Psychotherapy

Sara came into my life, and I into hers, at the right time. In the dog fancy world you will hear the term 'heart dog.' These are the ones that are most special to their owners. She was my heart dog and she gave love to others.

She was an extraordinary companion, and gave new meaning, to me, to the term 'companion animal.' My special relationship to her, and going through the loss of her, remained a private experience much like any other personal ones we have as psychoanalysts. What was different was that I shared my beloved companion animal with my patients. The inspiration for this paper came from my need to give her credit for the role she had in the treatment of my patients and in opening my eyes to this resource in private practice.[1]

I don't think I could say it any better myself.

Figure 16.1 Meika

The client reflections in Chapter 15 and the excerpt above appear to substantiate the earlier assertions in Chapter 3 regarding the many reasons why and how animal-assisted psychotherapy (AAP) is helpful. These include but are not limited to the following therapeutic roles that the therapy dogs play:

---

[1] Sacks (2008, p. 520).

1) The therapist appears less threatening when a friendly furry facilitator is present. Thus, the therapy dog helps to put clients at ease and to be cooperative.[2]

2) The therapy dog acts as an icebreaker and helps to establish the relationship between client and therapist.[3]

3) The therapy dog can help people feel less self-conscious and more comfortable around the therapist.[4]

4) Therapy dogs provide unconditional positive regard, love, and mutual acceptance of the client.[5]

5) Clients can satisfy a need for love/affection when they touch/pet/cuddle the animal.[6]

6) The therapist and therapy dog can act as role models.[7]

7) Therapy dogs can demonstrate appropriate, healthy boundaries.

8) Clients, especially children, may regulate their behavior when animals are present.

9) Clients may project their feelings onto the dog, which can allow the therapist to bring those feelings into the clients' awareness.[8]

---

[2] Chandler (2005, 2012); Delta Society (2000); Fine (2010); Hanselman (2001); Levinson (1997).

[3] Fine (2010); Wilkes (2009).

[4] Chandler (2005, 2012); Delta Society (2000); Fine (2010); Levinson (1997).

[5] Chandler (2005, 2012); Fine (2010); Geist (2011); Wilkes (2009).

[6] Chandler (2005, 2012); Fine (2010).

[7] Delta Society (2000).

[8] Chandler (2005, 2012); Fine (2010).

Figure 16.2 Loki

10) The therapy dog acts as an intermediary.[9]

11) When a client demonstrates anger or wanting to harm the dog, the therapist can respond with, "what is it that the dog is doing that promotes that thought/feeling/behavior," and then refer that back to the client's problems/behaviors/thoughts.

12) Negative reactions to therapy dogs, especially fear reactions, can lead to the processing of irrational fears.

13) The dog's behavior can serve to jump-start a discussion of human behaviors, such as sex, cleanliness, relationships, and so forth.[10]

---

[9] Ibid.
[10] Ibid.

14) When a therapy dog retires or dies, this event can be used for the process of working through grief or reactions to separation, abandonment, or death.[11]

I also think that our furry facilitators help our clients in many other ways, such as lifting their spirits when upset, providing a safe "object" with which to process difficult experiences when they cannot share with a human, even a safe person such as a counselor, and numerous other ways.

I also know that my therapy dogs offer me comfort and guidance, and they teach me to be humble and patient. They also help when they react in ways that I cannot, such as allowing a client to touch and to hug them or reacting to strong emotions in ways that facilitate the client's process of change.

Figure 16.1 Hobbes and Zoey

---

[11] Chandler (2005, 2012); Delta Society (2005); Geist (2011); Fine (2010); Levinson (1997).

In conclusion, I believe I have shown in the above-noted reflections and foregoing chapters that AAP is a very powerful and useful modality for clients' growth and well-being. When therapists use AAP as part of their orientations or modalities, clients and therapists can achieve treatment goals faster and in safer ways, and they can bring hidden issues to light so that they can explore and work through them for the benefit of clients.

Appendix

RESOURCES

ADA information:

http://www.ada.gov/qasrvc.htm
http://www.ada.gov/svcabrs3.pdf
http://www.ada.gov/regs2010/titleIII_2010/titleIII_2010
_withbold.htm

Connecticut State Law governing AAA/T:

http://www.cga.ct.gov/2013/FC/2013HB-06465-
R000802-FC.htm

Dogs for Diabetics:

http://www.dogs4diabetics.com/aboutus/aboutus.html
Dogs for First Line Responders, including Military:
http://companionsforheroes.org/

Dog Trainers:

Association of Pet Dog Trainers
101 North Main Street, # 610
Greenville, South Carolina 29601
(800) 738-3647
http://www.apdt.com

International Association of Canine Professionals
P.O. Box 560156
Montverde, Florida 34756
(407) 469-02008
http://www.dogpro.org

Fire Dogs: http://www.dhses.ny.gov/ofpc/

Guide and Hearing Dogs:
www.guidedogsofamerica.org
http://www.assistancedogsinternational.org/hearing.php

Military Dogs: http://www.militaryworkingdogs.com/

Obedience Certification for Dogs:

American Kennel Club – Canine Good Citizen test:
http://www.akc.org/events/cgc/training_testing.cfm

Patriot Service Dogs:
http://www.patriotservicedogs.org/
http://petsforpatriots.org/

Physical Assistance Dogs:
http://www.cci.org/site/
http://www.pawswithacause.org/

Police Service Dogs:
http://www.uspcak9.com/

Search and Rescue Dogs:
http://www.nasar.org/nasar/specialty_fields.php.

Seizure Alert Dogs:
http://www.epilepsyfoundation.org/

Therapy Dog Certification Agencies:

American Kennel Club (AKC) Headquarters
260 Madison Avenue
New York, New York 10016
(212) 696-8200
http://www.akc.org

Delta Society
875 124th Avenue Northeast, Suite 101
Bellevue, Washington 98005
(425) 679-5500
http://www.deltasocjety.org

Therapy Dogs International Inc. (TDI)
88 Bartley Road
Flanders, New Jersey 07836
(973) 252-9800
http://www.tdi-dog.org/

Therapy Dogs Inc.
P.O. Box 20227
Cheyenne, Wyoming 82003
(877) 843-7364
http://www.therapydogs.com

Therapy Dog Organizations by State:

ALABAMA

Hand-in-Paw, Inc.
5342 Oporto Madrid Blvd. So
Birmingham, AL 35210
(205) 591-7006
Fax: (205) 322-7784
E-mail: handinpawinc@aol.com
http://www.handinpaw.org/

Therapy Partners, Inc.
1015 A Cleaner Way
Huntsville, AL 35805
(256) 881-5700
http://www.therapypartners.org/

ARIZONA

Companion Animal Association of Arizona
Box 5006
Scottsdale, AZ 85261-5006
(602) 258-3306
http://www.caaainc.org/

Gabriel's Angels
1550 E. Maryland Ave., Suite 1
Phoenix, AZ 85014
(602) 266-0875
E-mail: info@petshelpingkids.com
http://www.gabrielsangels.org/

Pets on Wheels of Scottsdale
7375 E. 2nd St.
Scottsdale, AZ 85251
(480) 488-2002
Fax: (480) 312-1701
E-mail: petsonwheels@aol.com
http://www.petsonwheelsscottsdale.com/

Pet VIP
The Humane Society of Southern Arizona
3450 N. Kelvin Blvd.
Tucson, AZ 85716
(520) 321-3704 X 176
email: jspencer@humane-so-arizona.org
http://www.hssaz.org/site/PageServer?pagename=dogtra
ining_petVIP

ARKANSAS

Arkansas Hospice Foundation
Arkansas Hospice Pet Therapy
14 Parkstone Circle
North Little Rock, AR 72116
(501) 748-3333
(877) 713-2348
http://www.arkansashospice.org/foundation/volunteer_f
urryangels.html

Pet Therapy Program
City of Hot Springs
133 Convention Boulevard
Hot Springs National Park, AR 71901
(501) 760-7362
E-mail: info@cityhs.net
www.hotspringspettherapy.com

CALIFORNIA

Assistance Dog Institute
5860 Labath Avenue
Rohnert Park, CA 94928
(707) 545-3647
E-mail: info@berginu.edu
http://www.berginu.edu/

Furry Friends Pet Assisted Therapy Services
P.O. Box 5099
San Jose, CA 95150-5099
(877) 433-7287
(408) 629-8514
http://www.furryfriends.org/index.html

High Desert Obedience Club
Pet Pals
P.O. Box 2901
Lancaster, CA 93539
(661) 266-7097
E-mail: therapy@highdesertobedienceclub.org
http://www.highdesertobedienceclub.org/pages/therapy.
htm

Humane Society of Sonoma County
Pet Assisted Therapy
5345 Highway 12 West
Santa Rosa, CA 95407
(707) 542-0882 ext. 283
http://www.sonomahumane.org/community/pet_assisted
_therapy.html

Latham Foundation
1826 Clement Avenue
Alameda, CA 94501
(510) 521-0920
FAX: (510) 521-9861
E-mail: info@latham.org
http://www.latham.org/

Lend a Heart Inc.
P.O. Box 60617
Sacramento, CA 95860
E-mail: lendaheart.aat@gmail.com
http://www.lendaheart.org

Love on a Leash: The Foundation for Pet-Provided
Therapy
P.O. Box 4115
Oceanside, CA 92052
(760) 740-2326
info@loveonaleash.org
http://www.Loveonaleash.org

Loving Animals Providing Smiles
3366 Twin Oaks Drive
Napa, CA 94558
(707) 253-8585
E-mail: info@lovinganimalsprovidingsmiles.org
http://www.lovinganimalsprovidingsmiles.org/

Marin Humane Society
SHARE Program - Animal-Assisted Therapy
171 Bel Marin Keys Blvd.
Novato, CA 94949
(415) 883-4621
FAX: (415) 382-1349
E-mail: SHARE@marinhumanesociety.org
http://www.marinhumanesociety.org/site/c.aiIOI3NLKg
KYF/b.7727643/k.65C4/AnimalAssisted_Therapy.html

Ohlone Humane Society
Animal-Assisted Therapy Program
PMB #108, 39120 Argonaut Way
Fremont, CA 94538-1304
(510) 792-4587
E-Mail Ohlonehumane@aol.com
http://www.ohlonehumanesociety.org/info/display

Orange County Society for the Prevention of Cruelty to
Animals PAWS (Pets Are Wonderful Support)
P.O. Box 6507
Huntington Beach, CA 92615
(714) 964-4445
E-mail: info@orangecountyspca.org
http://orangecountyspca.org/program/paws/

Paws and Hearts
74-854 Velie Way, Suite 7
Palm Desert, CA 92260
(760) 836-1406
Fax: (760) 836-1426
E-email: pawsandhearts@aol.com
http://www.pawsandhearts.org/

Paws For Healing
1370 Trancas St
PMB 127
Napa, CA 94558
(707) 258-3846
E-mail: info@pawsforhealing.org
http://www.pawsforhealing.org/

PAWS - Pets are Wonderful Support
3170 23rd St
San Francisco, CA 94110
(415) 979-9550
FAX: (415) 979-9269
E-mall: info@pawssf.org
http://www.pawssf.org/

S.M.A.R.T. Dogs, Inc.
8019 Bristol Road
Dublin, CA 94586-1642
E-mail to cday25@aol.com
http://www.smartdogs.org/

San Francisco SPCA
Animal-Assisted Therapy Program
201 Alabama St.
San Francisco, CA 94103
(415) 554-3000
E-mail: public_info@sfspca.org
http://www.sfspca.org/programs-services/animal-
assisted-therapy

TherapyPets
P.O. Box 32288
Oakland, CA 94604
(510) 287-9042
FAX: (510) 893-0337
E-mail: gabbro@well.com
http://www.therapypets.org/

COLORADO

ANGEL Pups
Delta County, CO
(970) 874-0111
E-mail: mnbworrell@webtv.net

Cadence Center for Therapeutic Riding
P.O. Box 9009
Durango, CO 81301
(970) 749-7433
http://www.cadenceriding.org
info@CadenceRiding.org

The Children's Hospital Prescription Pet Program
13123 East 16th Avenue
Aurora, CO 80045
(720) 777-1234
http://www.childrenscolorado.org/give/volunteer/pet.as
px

Colorado Boys Ranch
P.O. Box 681
La Junta, CO 81050
(719) 384-5981
(800) 790-4993
Fax: (719) 384-8119
info@cbryouthconnect.org
http://www.coloradoboysranch.org

OR

14143 Denver West Parkway, Suite 100
Golden, CO 80401
(303) 691-6095
Fax: (303) 384-0020
info@youthconnect.org
http://www.coloradoboysranch.org

Foothills Animal Shelter
Pet Therapy Program
580 McIntyre Street
Golden, CO 80228
(303) 278-7575
Fax: (303) 278-8552
info@fas4pets.org
http://www.foothillsanimalshelter.org

CONNECTICUT

Tails of Joy Animal-Assisted Therapy Group
9 Iron Gate Lane
Cromwell, CT 06416
http://www.tailsofjoy.org/pages/about.htm

DELAWARE

Paws for People
P.O. Box 9955
Newark, DE 19714
(302) 351-5622
Fax (302) 351-8116
PAWSinfo@pawsforpeople.org
http://www.pawsforpeople.org

FLORIDA

Sarasota Manatee Association for Riding Therapy (SMART)
4800 CR 675
Brandenton, FL 34206
(941) 322-2000
http://www.smartriders.org

Sunshine on a Leash
1160 Duval Street
Jupiter, FL 33458
(772) 359-9797

OR

453 Caravelle Drive
Jupiter, FL 33458
(561) 776-8237
E-mail: info@sunshineonaleash.org
http://www.sunshineonaleash.org/index.htm

Tallahassee TheraPETics, Inc.
5405 Trinidad Drive
Tallahassee, FL 32310

Space Coast Therapy Dogs
P.O. Box 121474
West Melbourne, FL 32912
(321) 639-7323
http://www.spacecoasttherapydogs.org/index.htm

Hug A Pet of Pasco County
8809 Village Mill Row
Port Richey, FL 34667-2691
(727) 868-7057

GEORGIA

Dreamworkers, Inc.
4704 Brownsville Road
Powder Springs, GA 30127
E-mail: dreamworkers@bellsouth.net
http://www.dogsaver.org/dreamworkers/index.html

Happy Tails Pet Therapy, Inc.
P.O. Box 767961
Roswell, GA 30076
(770) 740-8211
FAX: (770) 740-6113
E-mail: info@happytailspets.org
http://www.happytailspets.org/index.php

HAWAII

Therapaws of Hawaii, dba Pa'ani Na Keiki
1198 Ikena Circle
Honolulu, HI 96821
(808) 377-3087
(808) 422-1920
E-mail: cgoldblatt@assets-school.net

ILLINOIS

People, Animals, Nature, Inc (PAN)
1820 Princeton Circle
Naperville, IL 60565
(630) 369-8328
E-mail: pan@pan-inc.org

Rainbow Animal-Assisted Therapy
6042 West Oakton Street
Morton Grove, IL 60053
(773) 283-1129
FAX: (847) 581-0233
E-mail: rainbowaat@gmail.com
http://www.rainbowaat.org/

SIT STAY READ!
811 W. Evergreen, Ste. 202
Chicago, IL 60642
(312) 573-8007
Email: info@sitstayread.org.
http://sitstayread.org/about/

KANSAS

Human Animal Bond Program
P.O. Box 3101
Ft. Leavenworth, KS 66027
(913) 684-6510
http://www.ftlcavenworthhab.net/

KENTUCKY

W.A.G.S. Pet Therapy of Kentucky, Inc.
P.O. Box 43504
Louisville, KY 40253
(502) 562-9247
http://www.kywags.org/

LOUISIANA

Visiting Pet Program
P.O. Box 24748
New Orleans, LA 70184-4748
(504) 432-8349
FAX: (815) 572-0177
E-mail: paws4visits@gmail.com
http://www.visitingpetprogram.org/

MARYLAND

Fidos For Freedom, Inc.
1200 Sandy Spring Rd
Laurel, MD 20707
(410) 880-4178
(301) 490-4005
FAX: (301) 490-9061
http://www.fidosforfreedom.org/

Pets On Wheels (this agency is in different counties in Maryland)
P.O. Box 44176
Baltimore, MD 21236

(410) 913-5569
FAX: (410) 256-0171
http://www.petsonwheels.org/

MASSACHUSETTS

Caring Canines (Boston, Massachusetts area pet therapy program)
(781) 729-8285
E-mail: Info@caringcanines.org
http://www.caringcanines.org/

Dog B.O.N.E.S. - Dogs Building Opportunities for Nurturing and Emotional Support
38 Garden Rd.
Scituate, MA 02066
(781) 264-5537
E-mail: dogbonestherapydogs@comcast.net17
http://www.therapydog.info/

Pets and People Foundation
49 Cottage St.
Watertown, MA 02472
(617) 600-4670
info@)petsandpeoplefoundation.org
http://www.petsandpeoplefoundation.org/

MICHIGAN

AnimaLink
(248) 770-5500
E-mail: info@animalink.com
http://www.animalink.com/AnimaLinkLLCWeb_files/A
AAT.htm

The Fur Angels
2984 Fort Street
Lincoln Park, MI 48146
(313) 289-4731
E- mail: hallshalfacre@aol.com
http://www.thefurangels.org/

MINNESOTA

Bark Avenue on Parade, Inc.
5205 29TH AVE S
Minneapolis, MN 55417-2001
E-mail: info@barkavenue.org
http://www.barkavenue.org/

Caring Critters of MN, Inc.
2254 Lilac Lane
White Bear Lake, MN 55110-3871
(651) 762-1581
E-mail: COuhl@email.msn.com
Puppy Love Therapy Dogs, Inc.
57240 Juniper Rd
Good Thunder, MN 56037
(507) 278-3488

E-mail: pltdi@hickorytech.net
http://puppylovetherapydogs-ivil.tripod.com/

Twin Cities Tail-Waggers Visiting Dog Group
Twin Cities Obedience Training Club
2101 Broadway, NE
Minneapolis, MN
(651) 762-1581
E-mail: Couhl@email.msn.com
http://www.tcotc.com/

MISSISSIPPI

Pets and People: Companions in Therapy and Service
P.O. Box 4266
Meridian, MS 39307
(601) 483-8970
E-mail: petsandpeople@geocities.com

MISSOURI

Support Dogs, Inc.
11645 Lilburn Park Rd.
St. Louis, MO 63146
(314) 997-2325
http://www.supportdogs.org/

NEBRASKA

Lincoln Pet Partners Inc.
1724 Trelawney Dr.

Lincoln, NE 68512-1828
(402) 423-3596
http://www.geocities.ws/lincolnpetpartners/how.html

Midlands Pet Therapy
5111 Grant Street
Omaha, NE 68104-4354
(402) 561-0550
E-mail: midlandspettherapy@gmail.com
http://www.midlandspettherapy.com/

Paws For Friendship, Inc.
P.O. Box 12243
Omaha, NE 68152
(402) 573-5826

NEW HAMPSHIRE

Caring Animal Partners
P.O. Box 1304
New London, NH 03257
(603) 927-4046
E-mail: nhcap@tds.net
http://www.caringanimalpartners.org/

NEW JERSEY

The Bright & Beautiful Therapy Dogs, Inc.
80 Powder Mill Road
Morris Plains, NJ
(888) 738-5770

E-mail: info@golden-dogs.org
http://www.golden-dogs.org/

TheraPet, Inc.
P.O. Box 787
Clark, NJ 07066
(732) 340-0728
E-mail: info@therapett-inc.com
http://www.therapet-inc.com/Mainpage.htm

NEW YORK

The Good Dog Foundation
P.O. Box 1484
New York, NY 10276
(888) 859-9992
E-mail: info@thegooddogfoundation.org
http://thegooddogfoundation.org/

OKLAHOMA

Petworks In Progress Foundation
P.O. Box 6282
Norman, OK 73070-6282
(405) 364-1525

OREGON

Furry Friends Foundation, Inc.
P.O. Box 698
Sisters, OR 97759
(541) 549-9941

E-mail: info@furryfriendsfoundation.org
http://furryfriendsfoundation.org/

Welcome Waggers Therapy Dogs
22830 Alsea Hwy
Philomath, OR 97370
(541) 929-5064
E-mail: k9calling@yahoo.com
http://www.welcomewaggers.org/

PENNSYLVANIA

Comfort Caring Canines Therapy Dogs, Inc.
2701 Valley Woods Road
Hatfield, PA 19440
(800) 331-4199
E-mail: ccc@comfortcaringcanines.org
http://comfortcaringcanines.org/wpp/

K-9 Partners: Therapy Dog, Support Dog & Service Dog
Training
334 Faggs Manor Road
Cochranville, PA 19330
(610) 869 4902
E-Mail: info@k94life.org
http://k94life.org/getadog/servicedog/
Lebanon County Kennel Club
P.O. Box 66
Palmyra, PA 17078
(717) 273-8612
http://lebanoncountykc.org/Site/Home.html

Lehigh Valley K-9 Therapy Association
Chapter 100 of Therapy Dogs International, Inc.
P.O. Box 208
Nazareth, PA 18064
(610) 759-2141
http://www.preciouspetservices.com/Lehigh-Valley-K-9-
Therapy-Association_Clubs-Associations-Therapy-Dogs-
Training-NAZARETH-PA_P78526.html

Pals For Life
939 Radnor Road
Wayne, PA 19087
(610) 687-1101
E-mail: Paula@palsforlife.org
http://www.palsforlife.org/

Pleasure of Your Company Therapy Dogs
P.O. Box 143
Kutztown, PA 19530
(610) 435-6870
E-email: poycdogs@yahoo.com
http://www.poycdogs.org/

SOUTH CAROLINA

SCDogs Therapy Group, Inc.
P.O. Box 12345
Sandy Springs, SC
(864) 287-1919
E-mail: info@SCDogs.org
http://www.scdogs.org/index.html

TENNESSEE

SMILE Program of Happy Tales Humane
230 Franklin Road
Suite 1303
Franklin, TN 37064
(615) 791-0827 ext. 11
E-mail: dcure@happytaleshumane.com
http://happytaleshumane.com/

Tender Paws
Pet Therapy of Clarksville, TN
Canine Hearts for the Community
Lori Finney, President
142 Kingswood Dr.
Clarksville, TN 37043
(931) 905-2648
http://www.tenderpawsclarksville.org/

TEXAS

Aggieland Pets With A Purpose
P.O. Box 10941
College Station, TX 77842
E-mail: information@apwap.org
http://www.apwap.org/

Faithful Friends Animal-Assisted Therapy Ministry
207 Briarwood Court
League City, TX 77573
(281) 488-2517

E-mail: shari@faithfulfriendsaat.com
http://www.faithfulfriendsaat.com/

Faithful Paws - Pet Therapy Program
Sponsored by: Bellaire United Methodist Church
4417 Bellaire Boulevard
Bellaire, TX 77401
(713) 666-2167
Fax: (713) 663-6397
E-mail: info@faithfulpawshouston.com
http://www.faithfulpawshouston.com/

Paws for Caring
5201 Memorial Drive, Suite PH 1162
Houston, TX 77007
(713) 840-7297
FAX: (713) 840-7205
E-mail: info@pawshouston.org
http://www.pawshouston.org/public/pag1.aspx
Therapet
P.O. Box 130118
Tyler, TX 75713
(903) 535-2125
FAX: (903) 535-2037
E-mail: therapetaat@gmail.com
http://www.therapet.com/

Therapy Pet Pals of Texas
3930 Bee Caves Rd
West Lake Hills, TX 78746
(512) 347-1984

E-mail: tppt_admin@therapypetpals.org
http://www.therapypetpals.org/

Therapy Tails on Wheels(c) 1995
AAA-AAT
Box 535
Kempner, TX 76539
E-mail:petmydog@vvm.com
http://therapytails.vze.com/

UTAH

InterMountain Therapy Animals
4050 South 2700 East
Salt Lake City, UT 84124
(801) 272-3439
FAX: (801) 272-3470
E-mail: info@therapyanimals.org
https://www.therapyanimals.org/Home.html

Therapy Animals of Utah
 2459 West 300 North
Provo, UT 84601
(801) 280-1855
E-mail: info@TherapyAnimalsUtah.org
http://www.therapyanimalsutah.org/

VERMONT

Therapy Dogs of Vermont
P.O. Box 1271
Williston, VT 05495-1271

E-mail: Admin@therapydogs.org
http://www.therapydogs.org/

VIRGINIA

Blue Grey Therapy Dogs
http://www.bluegraytherapydogs.org/

"Paws For Health" Pet Visitation Program
C/o Richmond SPCA
2519 Hermitage Road
Richmond, VA 23220
(804) 643-6785
E-mail: gbirdnecklace@richmondspca.org.
http://www.richmondspca.org/page.aspx?pid=832

WASHINGTON

Mtn Peaks Therapy Llamas & Alpacas
http://www.rojothellama.com/

Pawsitive Outreach
2704 N. Colville Rd.
Spokane, WA 99224
(509) 838-0596
Email: dlynndees@aol.com
http://www.lynndees.com/Pawsitive%20Outreach.html

The People-Pet Partnership
College of Veterinary Medicine
P.O. Box 647010

Washington State University
Pullman, WA 99164-7010
(509) 335-7347
Fax: (509) 335-6094
E-mail: sjacobson@vetmed.wsu.edu
http://www.vetmed.wsu.edu/depts-pppp/

Sirius Healing
Animal-Assisted Activities and Therapy Provider and
Trainer
12046 12th Avenue NE
Seattle, WA 98125-5014
(206) 363-3004
http://www.siriushealing.com/

Therapy DOGS ON CALL, an Easter Seals program
5960 East Shirley Lane
Montgomery, AL 36117
(334) 395-4489
http://www.dogsoncall.com/

WISCONSIN

Health Heelers, Inc.
Menomonee Falls, WI
(262) 442-9633
info@healthheelers.com
http://www.healthheelers.com/

Pets Helping People, Inc.
10150 W. Nash Street
Wauwatosa, WI 53222-2333

(414) 393-1111
FAX: (414) 393-1111
E-mail: petshelpingpeople@att.net
http://www.petshelpingpeople.org/

Therapy Dog Organizations, National and International:

Human Animal Interaction, Section 13 of Division 17 of the APA:
http://www.apa.org/divisions/div17/sections/sec13/Home.html

International Association of Human-Animal Interaction Organizations:
IAHAIO Secretary
Dr. Andrea M. Beetz
Department of Special Education
Institut für Sonderpädagogische Entwicklungsförderung und Rehabilitation University of Rostock
August-Bebel-Str.28
18055 Rostock
Germany
+49 9131 4000 455
+49 1762 3995 122
info@iahaio.org
http://www.iahaio.org/

Therapy Dog College/Certificate Programs:

Animal Behavioral Institute:
4711 Hope Valley Road
Suite 4F-332
Durham, North Carolina 27707
(866) 755-0448
support@animaledu.com
http://www.animaledu.com/Programs/AnimalAssistedT herapy.aspx

American Humane Society:
Animal-Assisted Therapy Program
63 Inverness Drive East
Englewood, Colorado 80112
(303) 792-5333
http://www.americanhumane.org/interaction/

Carol College, Montana:
Anthrozoology (Human-Animal Bond Program)
1601 N. Benton Ave
Helena, MT 59625
(800) 992-3648 or (406) 447-4300
http://www.carroll.edu/academics/majors/hab/

Oakland University:
Animal-Assisted Therapy
Suite 3027 Human Health Building
2200 N. Squirrel Road
Rochester, Michigan 48309-4401

nrsinfo@oakland.edu

Advising: (248) 370-4253

http://www.oakland.edu/animalassistedtherapy

University of Denver:

Animal-Assisted Social Work Certificate

2148 South High Street

Denver, Colorado 80208-7100

(303) 871-2886

Fax (303) 871-2845

http://www.du.edu/socialwork/programs/oncampus/tw
oyear/certificates/aaswcertificate.html

University of North Texas:

Center for Animal-Assisted Therapy

1155 Union Circle #310829

Denton, TX 76203-5017

(940) 565-2914

cynthia.chandler@unt.edu

http://www.coe.unt.edu/center-animal-assisted-therapy

Animal-Assisted Therapy Programs of Colorado:

1255 Lee Street

Lakewood, CO 80215

(720) 266-4444

 Fax: (720) 266-4444

info@aatpc.com

http://animalassistedtherapyprograms.com/

Professional Therapy Dogs of Colorado:

2121 S. Blackhawk St., Suite 210

Aurora, CO 80014

(720) 747-5584
Fax (866) 234-7181
Info@protherapydogscolorado.com
http://protherapydogscolorado.vpweb.com/?prefix=ww
w

Humane Society University, DC:
Animal-Assisted Intervention Graduate Certificate
Humane Society University
Attn: Office of Admissions
2100 L Street, NW
Washington, DC 20037
(202) 676-2390
Fax: (202) 778-6147
http://www.humanesocietyuniversity.org/academics/cas/
humaneleadership/aai-planofstudy.aspx

University of New Hampshire
Online course, search "animal" at:
http://www.learn.unh.edu/pcw/pd/sched-
id=30.php.html

U.S. Customs and Border Protection Dogs:
http://www.cbp.gov/xp/cgov/newsroom/fact_sheets/k9
_enforce/

References

Alers, E.V. & Simpson, K.V. (2012). Reclaiming identity through service to dogs in need. *The United States Army Medical Department Journal*, April-June, 70-73.

American Kennel Club. (2013). AKC's Canine Good Citizen. Retrieved March 24, 2013, from http://www.akc.org/events/cgc/training_testing.cfm.

American Psychological Association. (2003, 2010). Ethical Principles and Code of Conduct. Retrieved on March 2, 2013 from http://www.apa.org/ethics/code/principles.pdf.

Beck, C.E., Gonzales, F., Sells, C.H., Jones, C., Reer, T., Wasilewski, S., et al. (2012). The Effects of animal-assisted therapy on wounded warriors in an occupational therapy life skills program. *The United States Army Medical Department Journal*, April-June, 38-45.

Berry, A., Borgi, M., Francia, N., Alleva, E. & Cirulli, F. (2012). Use of assistance and therapy dogs for children with autism spectrum disorders: A critical review of the current evidence. *Journal of Alternative and Complementary Medicine*, 18, 1–8.

Blum Barish, E. (2002). Pets: Unconditional love. *Current Health*, 29(3), 16-17.

Bowlby, J. (1982). *Attachment* (2nd Edition). New York, NY: Basic Books.

Burch, M.R. (1996). *Volunteering with your pet: How to get involved in Animal-Assisted Therapy with any kind of pet.* New York, NY: Routledge, Howell Book House.

Butler, K. (2004). *Therapy Dogs Today: Their gifts, our obligation.* Norman, OK: Funpuddle Publishing Associates.

Capuzzi, J. (2004). Cuddle with Care. *Time International* (South Pacific Edition), 7, 63.

Cats, dogs, and other medicine. (2009, June 10). *Consumer Reports on Health.*

Center for Disease Control (2010). *Campylobacter infection and animals.* Retrieved March 2, 2013 from http://www.cdc.gov/healthypets/diseases/campyl obacterosis.htm.

Center for Disease Control (2010). *Cryptosporidium infection and animals.* Retrieved March 2, 2013 from http://www.cdc.gov/healthypets/diseases/cryptos poridiosis.htm.

Center for Disease Control (2010). *Yersinia enterocolitica and pigs.* Retrieved March 2, 2013 from http://www.cdc.gov/healthypets/diseases/yersini a.htm.

Chandler, C.K. (2005). *Animal-Assisted Therapy in Counseling.* New York, NY: Routledge, Taylor and Francis Group.

Chandler, C.K. (2012) *Animal-Assisted Therapy in Counseling* (2nd Ed.). New York, NY: Routledge, Taylor and Francis Group.

Chandler, C.K., Portrie-Bethke, T.L., Barrio Minton, C.A., Fernando, D.M., & O'Callaghan, D.M. (2010). Matching animal-assisted therapy techniques and intentions with counseling guiding theories. *Journal of Mental Health Counseling,* 32(4), 354-374.

Chomel, B.B. & Sun, B. (2011). Zoonoses in the bedroom. *Emerging Infectious Diseases*, 17(2), 26-31.

Chumley, P.R. (2012). Historical perspectives of the human-animal bond within the department of defense. *The United States Army Medical Department Journal*, April-June, 18-20.

Conrad, R.J. (1998). *Stubby the Military Dog: Stubby, Brave Soldier Dog of The 102nd Infantry*. Retrieved January 27, 2013, from http://www.ct.gov/mil/cwp/view.asp?a=1351&q =257892.

Delta Society. (2000). *The Pet Partners® Team Training Course Manual*. Reston, WA: Delta Society.

Delta Society. (2008). *The Pet Partners® Team Training Course Manual*. Reston, WA: Delta Society.

Delta Society (2012). *The Pet Partners® Team Training Course Manual*. Reston, WA: Delta Society.

Dodds, W.J. (2008). Shared infections. *Natural Wellness*, August, 16-17.

Đorđević, J., Tasić, S., Miladinović-Tasić, M. & Tasić, A (2010). Diagnosis and clinical importance of human dirofilariosis. *Scientific Journal of the Faculty of Medicine in Niš*, 27(2), 81-84.

Eggiman, J. (2006). Cognitive-Behavioral Therapy: A Case Report - Animal-Assisted Therapy. *Medscape* . Retrieved October 25, 2012, from http://www.medscape.com/viewarticle/545439.

Fike, L., Najera, C., & Dougherty, D. (2012). Occupational therapists as dog handlers: The collective experience with animal-assisted therapy in Iraq. *The United States Army Medical Department Journal*, April-June, 51-54.

Fine, A. H. (Ed.). (2010). *Handbook on animal-assisted therapy: Theoretical foundations and guidelines for practice* (3rd Ed.). London, UK: Academic Press.

Foreman, K. & Crosson, C. (2012). Canines for combat veterans: The national education for assistance dog services. *The United States Army Medical Department Journal*, April-June, 61-62.

Friesen, L. (2010). Exploring Animal-Assisted Programs with Children in School and Therapeutic Contexts. *Journal of Early Childhood Education*, 37, 261–267.

Garfield, S.L. & Bergin, A.E. (1986). *Handbook of psychotherapy and behavior change* (3rd Ed.) United States: John Wiley & Sons, Inc.

Geist, T.S. (2011). Conceptual Framework for Animal-Assisted Therapy. *Child Adolescent Social Work*, 28, 243–256.

Glaser, D.A. (1998). Tinea Barbae: Man and beast. *New England Journal of Medicine*, 338(11), 735.

Glickauf-Hughes, C. & Wells, M. (2007). *Object relations psychotherapy: An Individualized and interactive approach to Diagnosis and Treatment*. Lanham, MD: Rowman & Littlefield Publishers, Inc.

Goldstein, E.G. (1995). *Ego psychology and social work in practice* (2nd Ed.). New York, NY: The Free Press.

Golin, M. & Walsh, T. (1994). Heal emotions with fur, feathers and love. *Prevention*, 46(12), 80-83.

Good Therapy.org. (2013). *Emotionally focused therapy.* Retrieved on July 14, 2013 from http://www.goodtherapy.org/emotionally-focused-therapy.html.

Grado, E.M. (2011). Dr. Fluffy: An In-depth look at Animal-Assisted Therapy. *Exceptional Parent*, 41(5), 12-13.

Gregg, B.T. (2012). Crossing the berm: An occupational therapist's perspective on animal-assisted Therapy in a deployed environment. *The United States Army Medical Department Journal*, April-June, 55-56.

Hanselman, J.L. (2001). Coping skills interventions with adolescents in anger management using animals in therapy. *Journal of Child and Adolescent Group Therapy*, 11(4), 159-195.

Herman, J. (1997). *Trauma and recovery*. New York, NY: Basic Books.

Jalongo, M. R. (2005). *"What are all these dogs doing at school?" Using therapy dogs to promote children's reading practice*. Retrieved October 26, 2012 from http://www.thefreelibrary.com/_/print/PrintArti cle.aspx?id=134311927.

Jalongo, M.R., Astorino, T., & Bomboy, N. (2004). Canine visitors: The influence of therapy dogs on young children's learning and well-being in classrooms and hospitals. *Early Childhood Education Journal*, 32(1), 9-16.

Johnson, R.A. (2011). Animal-assisted intervention in health care contexts. In P. McCardle, S. McCune, J. Griffin, and V. Maholmes (Eds.). *How animals affect us: Examining the influences of human–animal interaction on child development and human health* (pp. 183-192). Washington, DC, US: American Psychological Association.

Johnson, S.M. (2004). *The practice of emotionally focused couple therapy* (2nd Ed.). New York, NY: Taylor & Francis Group.

Johnson, S.M. (2005). *Emotionally focused couple therapy with trauma survivors: Strengthening attachment bonds.* New York, NY: Guildford Publications, Inc.

Kaduson, H.G. & Schaefer, C.E. (Eds.). (2000). *Short-term play therapy for children.* New York, NY: The Guildford Press.

King, L.M. (2007). *Animal-Assisted Therapy: A guide for professional counselors, school counselors, social workers, and educators.* Bloomington, IN: Author House.

Kinsley, J.S., Barker, S.B., & Barker, R. T. (2012). Research on benefits of canine-assisted therapy for adults in nonmilitary settings. *The United States Army Medical Department Journal*, April-June, 30-37.

Krol, W. (2012). Training the combat and operational stress control dog: An innovative modality for behavioral health. *The United States Army Medical Department Journal*, April-June, 46-50.

Lange, A.M., Cox, J.A., Bernert, D.J., & Jenkins, C.D. (2006). Is counseling going to the dogs? An Exploratory study related to the inclusion of an animal in group counseling with adolescents. *Journal of Creativity in Mental Health*, 2(2), 17-31.

Lefkowitz, C., Paharia, I., Prout, M., Debiak, D., & Bleiberg, J. (2005). Animal-Assisted Prolonged Exposure: A Treatment for Survivors of Sexual Assault Suffering Posttraumatic Stress Disorder. *Society and Animals* 13(4), 275-295.

Levenson, H. (1995). *Time-limited dynamic psychotherapy.* New York, NY: Basic Books.

Levinson, B.M. (1962). The dog as a "co-therapist." *Mental Hygiene*, 46, 59-65.

Levinson, B.M. (1997). *Pet-oriented child psychotherapy* (Rev. ed.) Springfield, IL: Charles C. Thomas Publisher, Ltd.

Lind, N. (2009). *Animal assisted therapy activities to motivate and inspire.* Lombard IL: PYOW Publishing Ink.

Mahoney, M.J. (1991). *Human change processes: The Scientific foundations of psychotherapy.* United States: Basic Books, Inc.

Marr, C.A., French, L., Thompson, D., Drum, L., Greening, G., Mormon, J., Henderson, I., & Hughes, C.W. (2000). Animal-assisted therapy in psychiatric rehabilitation. *Anthrozoös*, 13, 43-47.

Matuszek, S. (2010). Animal-Facilitated Therapy in Various Patient Populations: Systematic Literature Review. *Holist Nurse Practitioner*, 24(4), 187–203.

McConnell, P.B. (2002). *The other end of the leash: Why we do what we do around dogs.* New York, NY: Ballantine Books.

McNally, S.P. (2001). *Sandplay: A Sourcebook for play therapists.* Lincoln, NE: Writers Club Press.

McWilliams, N. (1999). *Psychoanalytic case formulation.* New York, NY: The Guildford Press.

Miller, J. (2010). *Healing companions: Ordinary dogs and their extraordinary power to transform lives.* Franklin Lakes, NJ: The Career Press, Inc.

Mills, J.T. & Yeager, A.F. (2012). Definitions of animals used in health care settings. *The United States Army Medical Department Journal*, April-June, 12-17.

Minatrea, N.B. & Wesley, M.C. (2008). Reality therapy goes to the dogs. *International Journal of Reality Therapy*, 28(1), 69-77.

Moore, B.E. & Fine, B.D. (Eds.). (1990). *Psychoanalytic terms & concepts*. Binghamton, NY: Vail-Ballou Press.

O'Callaghan, D.M. & Chandler, C.K. (2011). An exploratory study of animal-assisted interventions utilized by mental health professionals. *Journal of Creativity in Mental Health*, 6, 90–104.

Parish-Plass, N. (2008). Animal-Assisted therapy with children suffering from insecure attachment due to abuse and neglect: A Method to lower the risk of intergenerational transmission of abuse? *Clinical Child Psychology and Psychiatry*, 13(1), 7-30.

Parish-Plass, N. (Ed.). (2013). *Animal-assisted psychotherapy: Theory, issues, and practice*. West Lafayette, IN: Purdue University Press.

Parshall, D.P. (2003). Research and reflection: Animal assisted therapy in mental health settings. *Counseling and Values*, 48, 47-56.

Perry, D, Rubinstein, D. & Austin, J. (2012). Animal-assisted group therapy in mental health settings: An initial model. *Alternative and Complementary Therapies*, 18(4), 181-185.

Peters, S.L. (2011, January 18). Animals can assist in psychotherapy. *USA Today*, p.4.

Peterson, L. (1999). How puppy love is therapeutic: The miracle of Murphy. *Biography*, 3(8), 44-47, 110-111.

Pets Are Wonderful Support. (2009). *Safe pet guidelines*. Retrieved July 10, 2013 from http://www.pawssf.org/page.aspx?pid=463.

Pichot, T. (2012). *Animal-Assisted Brief Therapy: A solution focused approach* (2nd Ed). New York, NY: Routledge.

Pitts, J.L. (2005). Why animal assisted therapy is important for children and youth. *The Exceptional Parent,* 35(10), 38-9.

Preziosi, R.J. (1997, Spring). For your consideration: A pet assisted therapist facilitator code of ethics. *Latham Letter,* 18(2), 5-6. Retrieved on July 10, 2013 from http://www.latham.org/Issues/LL_97_SP.pdf#page-.

Price, J.P. (2007). Cognitive schemas, defence mechanisms and post-traumatic stress symptomatology. *Psychology and Psychotherapy: Theory, Research and Practice,* 80, 343–353.

Prothmann, A., Albrecht, K., Dietrich, S., Hornfeck, U., Stieber, S., & Ettrich, C. (2005). Analysis of child–dog play behavior in child psychiatry. *Anthrozoös,* 18(1), 43-58.

Prothmann, A., Bienert, M., & Ettrich, C. (2006). Dogs in child psychotherapy: Effects on state of mind. *Anthrozoös,* 19(3), 265-277.

Reichert, E. (1998). Individual counseling for sexually abused children: A Role for animals and storytelling. *Child and Adolescent Social Work Journal,* 15(3), 177-185.

Ritchie, E. C., & Amaker, R.J. (2012). The early years. *The United States Army Medical Department Journal,* April-June, 5-7.

Rovner, J. (2012). *Pet therapy: how animals and humans heal each other.* Retrieved May 3, 2012, from http://www.npr.org/blogs/health/2012/03/05/1 46583986/pet-therapy-how-animals-and-hum.

Rubenstein, D.A., (2012). Perspectives. *The United States Army Medical Department Journal*, April-June, 1-4.

Sabry, M.A. & Lofty, H.S. (2009). Captive dogs as reservoirs of some zoonotic parasites. *Research Journal of Parasitology*, 4(4), 115-122.

Sacks, A. (2008). The therapeutic use of pets in private practice. *British Journal of Psychotherapy*, 24(4), 501-521.

Salb, A L., Barkema, H.W., Elkin, B.T., Thompson, R.C.A., Whiteside, D.P., Black, S.R., Dubey, J.P., & Kutz, S.J. (2008). Dogs as sources and sentinels of parasites in humans and wildlife, northern Canada. *Emerging Infectious Diseases*, 14(1), 61-63.

Schultz, P.N., Remick-Barlow, G.A., & Robbins, L. (2007). Equine-assisted psychotherapy: a mental health promotion/intervention modality for children who have experienced intra-family violence. *Health and Social Care in the Community*, 15(3), 265–271.

Scully, M.L. (2011). Pets in the bedroom — Move over rover! *Travel Medicine Advisor*, July, 117 & 120.

Shubert, J. (2012a). Dogs and human health/mental health: from the pleasure of their company to the benefits of their assistance. *The United States Army Medical Department Journal*, April-June, 21-29.

Shubert, J. (2012b). Therapy dogs and stress management assistance during disasters. *The United States Army Medical Department Journal*, April-June, 74-78.

Skloot, R. (2008). *Creature Comforts*. Retrieved February 2, 2013 from http://www.nytimes.com/2009/01/04/magazine/04Creatures-t.html?_r=0&em=&pagewante.

Souter, M.A. & Miller, M.D., (2007). Do animal-assisted activities effectively treat depression? A Meta-analysis. *Anthrozoös*, 20(2), 167–181.

Taffel, R. (2005). *Breaking through to teens: A new psychology for the new adolescent*. New York, NY: Guildford Press.

Tartakovsky, M. (2011). *Emotionally focused therapy: Bolstering couples' emotional bonds*. Retrieved on July 14, 2013 from http://psychcentral.com/lib/2011/emotionally-focused-therapy-bolstering-couples-emotional-bonds/all/1/.

Tellington-Jones, L. (2012). *Getting in TTouch with your dog: A gentle approach to influencing behavior, health, and performance*. North Pomfret, VT: Trafalgar Square Books.

Teyber, E. (2000). *Interpersonal process in psychotherapy: A Relational approach* (4th Ed.). Belmont, CA: Wadsworth/Thomas Learning.

University of British Columbia, Okanagan. (2012). *A mutt called Frances helps teach students at UBC's Okanagan Campus*. Retrieved December 5, 2012 from http://www.castanet.net/news/Campus-Life/84082/A-mutt-called-Frances-helps-teach-stud.

Man and beast both at risk (2005). *U.S.A. Today, 134(2725)*, 16.

U.S. Department of Justice. (2002). *ADA Business Brief: Service Animals*. Retrieved January 27, 2013 from http://www.ada.gov/svcanimb.htm.

U.S. Department of Justice, Civil Rights Division. (2010). *Title III, Part 36. Nondiscrimination on the Basis of Disability in Public Accommodations and Commercial Facilities* (as amended by the final rule published in September 15, 2010), section 36.104 Definitions. Found at http://www.ada.gov/regs2010/titleIII_2010/titleIII_2010_withbold.htm.

Volhard, J. & Volhard, W. (2005). *Dog training for dummies* (2nd Ed). Hoboken, NJ: Wiley Publishing, Inc.

Walsh, F. (2009). Human-Animal bonds II: The Role of pets in family systems and family therapy. *Family Process*, 48, 481–499.

Warner, R.D. (1984). Occurrence and impact of zoonoses in pet dogs and cats at US Air Force bases. *American Journal of Public Health*, 74(11), 1239-1242.

Watkins, K.L. (2012). Policy Initiatives for the use of canines in army medicine. *The United States Army Medical Department Journal*, April-June, 8-11.

Wells, M.W., Glickauf-Hughes, C., & Beaudoin, P. (1995). An ego/object relations approach to treating childhood sexual abuse survivors. *Psychotherapy*, 32(3), 416-429.

Wilkes, J.K. (2009). *The role of companion animals in counseling and psychology: Discovering their use in the therapeutic process*. Springfield, IL: Charles C. Thomas Publisher, Ltd.

Yeager, A.F. & Irwin, J. (2012). Rehabilitative canine interactions at the Walter Reed National Military

Medical Center. *The United States Army Medical Department Journal*, April-June, 57-60.

Yount, R.A., Olmert, M.D., & Lee, M.R. (2012). Service dog training program for treatment of Posttraumatic stress in service members. *The United States Army Medical Department Journal*, April-June, 63-69.

Zamir, T. (2006). The moral basis of animal-assisted therapy. *Society & Animals*, 14(2), 179-199.

Zilcha-Mano, S., Mikulincer, M., & Shaver, P.R. (2011). Pet in the therapy room: An attachment perspective on Animal-Assisted Therapy. *Attachment & Human Development*, 13(6), 541-561.

INDEX